AMERICAN VOICES FROM

THE
New Republic
1783–1830

AMERICAN VOICES FROM

THE
New Republic
1783–1830

Rebecca Stefoff

BENCHMARK BOOKS

MARSHALL CAVENDISH
NEW YORK

FOR MY PARENTS

Benchmark Books
Marshall Cavendish
99 White Plains Road
Tarrytown, New York 10591-9001
www.marshallcavendish.com

Library of Congress Cataloging-in-Publication Data
Stefoff, Rebecca, 1951-
The new republic: 1783-1830 / by Rebecca Stefoff.
p. cm. — (American voices from—)
Includes bibliographical references and index.
ISBN 0-7614-1695-1
1. United States—Politics and government—1783-1865—Juvenile literature. 2. United States—Civilization—1783-1865—Juvenile literature. 3. United States—Politics and government—1783-1865—Sources—Juvenile literature. 4. United States—Civilization—1783-1865—Sources—Juvenile literature. I. Title. II. Series.

E302.1.S74 2005
973.4--dc22
2004011391

Printed in China
1 3 5 6 4 2

Series design and composition by Anne Scatto / PIXEL PRESS
Linda Sykes Picture Research, Inc., Hilton Head, S.C.

ON THE COVER: *Election Day 1815* by John Lewis Krimmel, an emigrant from Germany who became a well-known artist in the early years of the American republic.

ON THE TITLE PAGE: New Orleans as it looked at the time of the Louisiana Purchase, which added the busy Mississippi River port to the United States. The patriotic slogan above the port, held by a bird possibly meant to represent an eagle, reads in full "Under My Wings Every Thing Prospers."

Acknowledgments

The author is grateful to Zachary Harris of C/Z Harris Ltd. for research services that were not only helpful but essential in the preparation of this book.

Permission has been granted to use quotations from the following copyrighted works:

Extract from George Mason's speech from *Witnesses at the Creation: Hamilton, Madison, Jay and the Constitution* by Richard B. Morris. Copyright © 1985 by Richard B. Morris. Reprinted by permission of Henry Holt & Co., LLC.

Extract from *The World of Eli Whitney* by Jeannette Mirsky and Allen Nevins. Copyright © 1952 by Jeannette Mirsky and Allen Nevins; copyright renewed © 1980. Reprinted with permission of Scribner, a division of Simon & Schuster.

Extract from *A Journal by Thomas Hughes*, E. A. Benians, editor. Copyright © 1947 Cambridge University Press. Reprinted with the permission of Cambridge University Press.

Extract from Benjamin Rush, *The Autobiography of Benjamin Rush*, George W. Corner, editor. Copyright © 1948 by American Philosophical Society. Reprinted by permission of Princeton University Press.

A Note to the Reader

The pieces of history quoted in this book come from the pens of many different writers, some more educated and polished than others. Several hundred years ago, even educated people used spelling, grammar, and vocabulary words different from those of today. I have tried to explain terms that you might not recognize. Some of the spelling and punctuation you will see in these quotations may seem unusual to you. Ignore the strangeness and look for the meaning that lies beneath. Reading the words of the people who lived history is a window into the past—the closest thing to a time machine that we are ever likely to have.

I hope that these original writings from the days of the New Republic make you want to learn more about the people and events of this fascinating time. When a quote sparks your interest, read more by looking up the source from which it comes. You can also find more information about the era in the books and Web sites listed at the back of this book.

Contents

About Primary Sources   *ix*

Introduction: Birth of a Nation   *xv*

Chapter 1 | *Forming a New Government*   *1*

"This Melancholy State of Our Country": The Need for
a New Constitution   3

The Proper Role of Government: John Locke and the Enlightenment   5

John Adams on Democratic Government   8

"Near to Perfection": Benjamin Franklin on the Constitution   11

"The American Nation and Its Homeland": From *The Federalist*   14

An Anti-federalist's Advice: Mercy Otis Warren Speaks to
Future Americans   17

Chapter 2 | *Presidents and Parties*   *21*

George Washington's Farewell Address to the People of the United
States   24

James Madison Outlines Republican Views   26

Alexander Hamilton's Letter about the Virginia and Kentucky
Resolutions   29

A Bid for Unity: Thomas Jefferson's First Inaugural Address   31

Edward Everett on the Deaths of Adams and Jefferson   35

Chapter 3 | *International Affairs*   *38*

War in the Northwest Territory: A British Officer on the
American Frontier   40

Curses on the "Arch Traitor": Americans Respond to the Jay Treaty   43

War against the Barbary Pirates   45

An American Victory at Sea: The *Constitution* vs. the *Guerrière*   47

Policing the Americas: The Monroe Doctrine   50

Chapter 4 | American Affairs   53

A New Capital City: Thomas Jefferson on the Creation of Washington, DC   55
A Threat to Freedom of the Press: The Alien and Sedition Acts   57
Lewis and Clark Explore the West: Letter to the Oto Indians   59
"The Dangers of American Liberty"   62
The Supreme Court and States' Rights: John Marshall
    Hands Down an Opinion   63

Chapter 5 | African Americans and Slavery   68

A Southerner Condemns Slavery   71
David Walker Cries Out against Injustice   72
William Lloyd Garrison Crusades against Slavery   74
Born into Slavery: The Narrative of Moses Roper   76
A Midnight Escape: John Malvin Leads Slaves to Freedom   77

Chapter 6 | Arts and Sciences   81

Exploring for Science: William Bartram in Georgia   82
"Every thing that is curious of this Country": America's First Museum   85
Inventing Modern Industry: Eli Whitney's Cotton Gin   87
An Early American Play: Songs from *The Indian Princess*   88
Creating an American Hero: Natty Bumppo in *The Pioneers*   90

Chapter 7 | The Age of New Possibilities   93

"Those Active, Interesting Girls": The Women of the Lowell Factories   94
An Englishwoman Describes Americans: Frances Trollope   97
An Unusual Business: The Ice Trade   99
Catherine Beecher's Suggestions for Improving Education   102
"Unrivalled Work": Philip Freneau's Poem about the Erie Canal   104

Time Line   *108*
Glossary   *110*
To Find Out More   *111*
Index   *114*

Primary sources can be many things other than written texts—even money carries information. This coin, minted in 1782, shows that July 4, 1776, was already being honored as the date on which American independence was born. The slogan is Latin for "American Liberty."

About Primary Sources

What Is a Primary Source?

In the pages that follow, you will be hearing many different "voices" from a special time in America's past. Some of the selections are long and others are short. You'll find many easy to understand at first reading, while others may require several readings. All the selections have one thing in common, however. They are primary sources. This is the name historians give to the bits and pieces of information that make up the record of human existence. Primary sources are important to us because they are the core material of all historical investigation. You might call them "history" itself.

Primary sources are evidence; they give historians the all-important clues they need to understand the past. Perhaps you have read a detective story in which a sleuth must solve a mystery by piecing together bits of evidence he or she uncovers. The detective makes deductions, or educated guesses based on the evidence, and solves the mystery once all the deductions point in a certain direction. Historians work in much the same way. Like detectives, historians analyze data through careful reading and rereading. After much analysis, historians draw conclusions about an event, a person, or an entire era. Individual historians may analyze the same evidence and come to different conclusions. That is why there is often sharp disagreement about an event.

John Adams (1735–1826) in a 1766 portrait by Benjamin Blythe. Adams, who later served as vice president and president of the young republic, left a wealth of primary sources, including speeches, published writings, and many letters to family and friends.

Primary sources are also called *documents.* This rather dry word can be used to describe many different things: an official speech by a government leader, an old map, an act of Congress, a letter worn out from much handling, an entry hastily scrawled in a diary, a detailed newspaper account of an event, a funny or sad song, a colorful poster, a cartoon, an old painting, a faded photograph, or someone's remembrances captured on tape or film.

By examining the following documents, you the reader will be taking on the role of historian. Here is your chance to immerse yourself in what may be called the defining era of American history—the years following the Revolutionary War, when the United States

After Englishwoman Frances Trollope published a book critical of American culture and customs (see Chapter 7), this cartoon poking fun at Trollope and her two daughters appeared in the United States.

took its first steps as a republic. You will come to know not only the great statesmen and thinkers who founded the New Republic, but also the inventors, entrepreneurs, artists, and writers who shaped the young nation. You'll hear the voices of the disenfranchised as well—African Americans, both free and slave, who spoke out for equality in the new land of liberty; women who wrote and worked and had unusual thoughts about independence and self-respect.

Our language has changed since the late eighteenth and early nineteenth century. Some words and expressions will be unfamiliar to a person living in the twenty-first century. Even familiar words may have been spelled differently then. Don't be discouraged! Trying to figure out language is exactly the kind of work a historian does. Like a historian, you will end with a deeper, more meaningful understanding of the past.

How to Read a Primary Source

Each document in this book deals with some aspect of life in the New Republic, the period between 1783 and 1830. Some of the documents are from government archives or from the official papers of major historical figures. Others are taken from the letters and diaries that ordinary people wrote or from the pamphlets and newspapers that kept Americans informed. All of these documents help us to understand what it was like to live in the early years of the republic.

As you read each document, ask yourself some basic questions. Who is writing or speaking? What is the writer's point of view? Who is the writer's audience? What is he or she trying to tell the audience? Is the message clearly expressed, or is it implied, that is, stated indirectly? What words does the writer use to convey his or her message? Are the words emotional or objective in tone? If you are looking at a historical painting or other work of art, examine it carefully, taking in all the details. What is happening in the foreground? In the background? What is its purpose? These are questions that can help you think critically about a primary source.

Some tools have been included with the documents to help you in your investigations. Unusual words have been listed and defined near the selections. Thought-provoking questions follow each document. They help focus your reading so you can get the most out of the document. As you read each selection, you'll probably come up with many questions of your own. That's great! The work of a historian always leads to many, many questions. Some can be answered, while others require more investigation. Perhaps when you finish this book, your questions will lead you to further explorations in early American history.

The Constitution is probably the single most important primary source from the formative years of the United States. Far from a museum piece, it is still evolving and being interpreted today.

A key feature of the new American republic was pride in the events that had marked the nation's struggle for independence. These events— such as the ringing of the Liberty Bell at Independence Hall, Philadelphia, on July 4, 1776, shown here—quickly became part of the nation's mythology as well as its history.

Introduction

BIRTH OF A NATION

Beginning in the early seventeenth century, England established a string of colonies along the eastern coast of North America. In the mid-eighteenth century, the relationship between those colonies and their parent country became strained. Matters grew so bad that in the 1770s, the colonists took up arms to fight for their independence in what came to be called the American Revolution. England—by now known as Great Britain—could not keep its grip on the colonies. The Revolution ended in 1783 with the Treaty of Paris, which recognized the former colonies as a new nation—the United States of America. The colonists had won their freedom. Now they faced the great question: What would they do with it?

Ahead of the new nation lay many challenges. The most urgent concerned government, money, and international relations. Americans' responses to these early challenges would determine whether the United States would survive and what kind of nation it would become. In the course of dealing with the issues that arose in the forty years after the Revolution, Americans invented their country.

What kind of government would the newborn United States

have? Many of the former colonists had agreed on the need for independence, and they had fought side by side to achieve it. Once that war was won, however, those who had led the fight were not in complete agreement about how their country should govern itself. Everyone wanted the nation to be a republic—a country in which the people governed themselves through representatives whom they elected. The difficulty came in deciding what kind of a republic it should be. How should laws be made, and by whom? Who should have the power to declare war and to make peace? Who would decide how to spend the country's money? Should a single person serve as the head of state?

Before the Revolution, each colony had had some kind of governing body, although all of them were subject to British rule and had governors appointed by Great Britain. During the Revolution, the colonies became self-governing states. Each adopted a state constitution that explained how it would be governed. In addition, representatives of the states agreed to form a central government to carry out certain functions, such as war and diplomacy, on behalf of all the states. The result was the Articles of Confederation. Under this agreement, the thirteen states formed a loose association under a central government. That central government had limited powers— it could conduct relations with foreign powers and direct a national army, for example, but it could not supervise the states' trade with other countries or require citizens to join the army.

After the Revolution, the states had to decide whether to continue under the Articles of Confederation or try to develop a new central government. Some Americans wanted each state to remain a separate, independent nation, so that the United States would

really be thirteen countries, not one. Most people, however, realized that each state alone would be too weak and too small to defend itself against foreign powers or to build a strong economy. Just as the states had banded together of necessity to win the war, they now had to unite to prosper in peace. In 1787 the states sent representatives to the Constitutional Convention in Philadelphia to talk about changing the Articles of Confederation. From that meeting would be born a new constitution and a new national, or federal, government. Yet this important event created a deep split in the ranks of the country's leaders. On one side were those who favored a strong central government, on the other were those who favored strong state governments and

George Washington presides over a meeting of the Constitutional Convention in Philadelphia in 1787. This illustration is based on a painting by Virginia-born Junius Brutus Stearns (1810–1855), who depicted many historical scenes, including five of Washington at various times in his career.

limited central control. In time the split widened, giving rise to the nation's first political parties, which competed for influence and public office.

The problem of money went hand in hand with that of government. After the Revolution, the United States was broke and in debt. It owed money to Americans and to foreign countries—money it had borrowed to pay for the war and could not now repay. It also owed money to American soldiers—back pay that they had not received during the war. Eventually the nation's leaders would decide that the country's financial problems could best be solved by a federal government with the power to collect taxes from the citizens. The decision to strengthen the central government's financial powers led to more disputes between Federalists, who supported a strong federal government, and Anti-Federalists, or Republicans, who feared that such a government might overstep its rights.

In addition to planning its government and raising money, the new United States had to maintain relations with other nations. France had been an ally during the Revolution, but in the 1790s conflict arose between France and the United States. For several years the two nations fought openly, although war was never declared. A few years later the United States fought a war against North African pirates. But the most dramatic and important war in the young nation's early history began in 1812, once again pitting the United States against Great Britain. The United States defended itself well against British attacks and earned the respect of other nations. So powerful had it become that in 1823 the United States warned the nations of Europe not to try to

influence events or establish new colonies *any-where* in North, Central, or South America. Forty years after the Treaty of Paris, the United States had not only survived; it had become a world power.

American warships bombard the North African city of Tripoli in the War against the Barbary Pirates *(see Chapter 3)*, one of America's first foreign wars. The United States became an international power during the New Republic period.

One of the most significant features of that forty-year period was the formation of an American sense of identity. At the time of the Revolution, people thought of themselves as Virginians or New Yorkers, Northerners or Southerners, city folk or country people. Although they continued to define themselves in such terms, as time went on they came to think of themselves first and foremost as Americans.

Painter John Lewis Krimmel, who arrived in the United States from Germany in 1810, specialized in colorful, idealized scenes of public life. He created several very similar patriotic images of Election Day—compare this one to the one reproduced on the title page. Krimmel's work was very popular, and other artists imitated his style and subject matter well into the nineteenth century.

A web of shared memories, stories, and rituals knitted them together. Above all, they shared an exciting sense of being part of history—of being present when a new nation, *their* nation, came of age. Lucy Larcom grew up in Massachusetts in the early years of the nineteenth century. In her 1889 book, *A New England Girlhood,* she looked back on the patriotic enthusiasm of America's first decades, when heroes of the Revolution still strode the land:

> OUR REPUBLICANISM WAS fresh and wide-awake. The edge of George Washington's little hatchet had not yet been worn down to its latter-day dullness; it flashed keenly on our young eyes and ears in the reading books, and through Fourth of July speeches. The Father of his Country had been dead only a little more than a quarter of a century, and General Lafayette was still alive; he had, indeed, passed through our town but a few years before, and had been publicly welcomed under our own elms and lindens. Even babies echoed the names of our two great heroes in their prattle.
>
> We had great "training-days," when drum and fife took our ears by storm; when the militia and the Light Infantry mustered and marched through the streets to the Common, with boys and girls at their heels,—such girls as could get their mother's consent, or the courage to run off without it. We never could. But we always managed to get a good look at the show in one way or another.
>
> "Old Election," "'Lection Day" we called it, a lost holiday now, was a general training day, and it came at our most

delightful season, the last of May. . . . The Fourth of July and Thanksgiving Day were the only other holidays that we made much account of, and the former was a far more well-behaved festival than it is in modern times. The bells rang without stint, and at morning and noon cannon were fired off. But torpedoes and firecrackers did not make the highways dangerous;—perhaps they were thought too expensive an amusement. Somebody delivered an oration; there was a good deal said about "this universal Yankee nation"; some rockets went up from Salem in the evening; we watched them from the hill, and then went to bed, feeling that we had been good patriots.

Lucy Larcom, photographed around 1890, near the end of her life, left a vivid account of how citizens celebrated patriotic holidays during her childhood in the early years of the republic.

The patriotic enthusiasm of those early years was genuine, yet there was much strife and turmoil as well. Political life was torn by disagreements and bitter feuds. In the years immediately after the Revolution, economic depression gripped the land and drove some groups of citizens to rebel against the government or even to consider withdrawing from the United States. The country had to defend itself against two of the strongest nations in the world. The American victory in the Revolutionary War had been impressive, but America's real success story unfolded in the years that followed, as the citizens of the new republic forged a unified government, a growing economy, and the beginning of a truly American culture.

The signing of the United States Constitution on September 17, 1787, is a subject that has attracted many artists and illustrators over the years. This interpretation of the scene by Howard Chandler Christy (1873–1952) highlights recognizable figures such as George Washington (standing on the podium) and Benjamin Franklin (seated, with a cane).

Chapter I

Forming a New Government

THE CONSTITUTIONAL CONVENTION labored through Philadelphia's unusually hot summer of 1787. At times, tempers in the meeting rooms rose higher than the temperatures outside. Delegates to the convention disagreed about many things. Should the legislative (lawmaking) branch of government be a single body, or should it be composed of two groups? Should each state have the same number of representatives in the legislature, or should representation be based on a state's population? Should the Constitution, which was basically a plan for organizing a federal government, list the rights of citizens? And how would the federal government share power with the state governments that already existed? A few delegates even suggested that the states of the North and the South should form separate governments.

Eventually the convention reached agreement on these issues through a series of compromises in which each side gave up some of its demands. The result was a Constitution that most delegates thought was less than perfect but probably the best that could be achieved. The next step was to get the American people to accept it. To become law, the Constitution had to be ratified, or approved, by nine of the thirteen states. As the states organized special conventions to vote on the Constitution, those for and against the new plan tried to influence the public through newspaper articles, pamphlets, and speeches.

Those who supported the Constitution most were a group of political thinkers who believed that the new republic urgently needed a strong federal government, the kind that would be established under the Constitution. These Federalists, as they came to be called, included Alexander Hamilton, John Jay, George Washington, and Benjamin Franklin. Hamilton and Jay wrote a series of articles defending the proposed Constitution and the notion of federal government. These were later published under the title *The Federalist.*

On the other side of the debate were the Anti-Federalists, who feared that a strong central government might abuse its powers, even perhaps going so far as to limit the rights and freedoms of the people. Thomas Jefferson was fearful of too much federal power and thought that the states should retain more self-rule than the Constitution granted them. Another leading Anti-Federalist was Patrick Henry of Virginia, whose cry "Give me liberty or give me death!" had become a slogan of the Revolution. Henry felt that the move toward a strong federal government took too much power out of the hands of citizens and communities. He warned Americans to guard their liberties carefully for fear they should lose them forever.

Many people were troubled by the fact that the Constitution

did not specifically guarantee individual rights and freedoms. Several states refused to ratify the Constitution until the leading Federalists promised that Congress would immediately add to it a statement of rights.

By mid-1788 nine states had ratified the Constitution, but the two largest states, New York and Virginia, had not yet done so. Without their support, the new federal government would be weak from the start. Both states ratified the Constitution soon afterward, however. In 1789 North Carolina accepted the Constitution. Rhode Island followed the next year, making ratification complete. In 1791 Congress, as promised, passed a set of ten amendments, or changes, to the Constitution. These amendments, together called the Bill of Rights, list basic liberties that the federal government cannot take away from U.S. citizens. Among them are freedom of religion, freedom of speech and of the press, and the right to a speedy, public, and fair trial.

"This Melancholy State of Our Country": The Need for a New Constitution

Benjamin Rush of Philadelphia, a doctor and teacher of medicine, played an important role in the American fight for independence from Great Britain. One of the signers of the Declaration of Independence, Rush served as a surgeon in the colonists' Continental Army. Some years later he held the post of national treasurer. In an account of his life written for his children and descendants, Rush described the confusion of the 1780s and expressed his belief that the country needed a stronger central government.

THE SITUATION OF THE United States during this time was far from being an agreeable one. The weakness of the confederation . . . had limited the commerce of our country, and produced universal distress in our cities. In the year 1788 there were 1,000 empty houses in Philadelphia. Bricklayers and house carpenters and all the mechanics and labourers who are dependent upon them were unemployed. The value of property in and near the city was two-thirds less than before the year 1774. Bankruptcies were numerous and beggars were to be seen at the doors of the opulent in every street of our city. Taxes were heavy and subscriptions for the relief of the poor still more oppressive. In this melancholy state of our country it occurred to thinking men that all our evils originated in a weakness of the general government. These evils were pointed out in many publications in all the States, and a convention was finally called to correct the defect of the confederation. While we were sitting in the year 1787 I received a letter from Mr. Dickinson, who was a member of the convention, calling me to come forward in support of the proposed Constitution of the United States. I had heard enough of its form and principles to be satisfied

Dr. Benjamin Rush of Philadelphia was a leading figure in political life during the Revolutionary and New Republic eras. In 1797 President John Adams made Rush the U.S. treasurer, a position the patriotic physician held until his death in 1813.

". . .all our evils originated in a weakness of the general government."

with it, and readily obeyed the call of my friend by recommending and defending it in a number of addresses to the citizens of the United States. The zeal I had discovered in my publications and speeches at town meetings induced the citizens of Philadelphia to elect me a member of the convention that met in Pennsylvania to adopt or reject the proposed federal constitution. It was adopted by a vote of two-thirds of the convention. . . . I had resolved and repeatedly declared that I would close my political labors with the establishment of a safe and efficient general government. I considered this as an act of consistency, for to assist in making a people free, without furnishing them the means of preserving their freedom, would have been doing them more harm than good.

—*From Benjamin Rush,* The Autobiography of Benjamin Rush, *George W. Corner, editor. Princeton, NJ: Princeton University Press for the American Philosophical Society, 1948.*

THINK ABOUT THIS

1. What symptoms does Rush give of the country's sorry or "melancholy" state in the 1780s?
2. How did Rush become a member of the Constitutional Convention?

The Proper Role of Government: John Locke and the Enlightenment

The Enlightenment movement began in the late seventeenth century and continued into the eighteenth, a period sometimes called the Age of Reason. Among the thinkers of this period were the French philosophers René Descartes, Denis Diderot, Jean-Jacques Rousseau, and Voltaire. Enlightenment philosophers celebrated the power of reason, or clear and logical thought, as the best way to arrive at truth. Their thinking relied strongly on the scientific method, with its emphasis on careful observation and experimentation. Their work produced many advances in science—in fields such as anatomy, chemistry, astronomy, mathematics, and physics. It also greatly affected ideas about society, for the Enlightenment philosophers believed that the scientific method could be applied to the study of human nature. They analyzed issues in law, politics, and education and attacked tyranny, social injustice, superstition, and ignorance. They helped change English politics and society, provided an intellectual foundation for the American and French Revolutions, and had a profound effect upon the authors of the U.S. Constitution. Probably the most influential Enlightenment thinker was an Englishman: John Locke, whose *Two Treatises of Government* (1690) discussed the rights and responsibilities of governments and individuals. Many of Locke's ideas found their way into the document prepared by the Constitutional Convention.

IF MAN IN THE STATE OF NATURE be so free, as has been said, if he be absolute lord of his own person and possessions, equal to the greatest, and subject to nobody, why will he part with his freedom, why will he give up his empire and subject himself to the dominion and control of any other power? To which it is obvious to answer that though in the state of nature he hath such a right, yet the enjoyment of it is very uncertain and constantly exposed to the invasion of others; for all being kings as much as he, every man his equal, and the greater part no strict observers of equity and justice, the enjoyment of the property he has in this state is very unsafe, very unsecure. This makes him willing to quit a condition which, however free, is full of fears and continual dangers; and it is not without reason that he seeks out and is willing to join in society with others who are already united, or have a mind to unite, for the mutual preservation of their lives, liberties, and estates, which I call by the general name "property."

The great and chief end, therefore, of men's uniting into commonwealths and putting themselves under government is the preservation of their property. . . .

But though men when they enter into society give up the equality, liberty, and executive power they had in the state of nature into the hands of the society, to be so far disposed of by the legislative as the good of the society shall require, yet it being only with an intention in every one the better to preserve himself, his liberty and property—for no rational creature can be supposed to change his

English philosopher John Locke (1632–1704) helped usher in Europe's Enlightenment, or Age of Reason. His ideas about the rights and responsibilities of government are reflected in the U.S. Constitution.

condition with an intention to be worse—the power of the society, or legislative constituted by them, can never be supposed to extend farther than the common good. . . . And so whoever has the legislative or supreme power of any commonwealth is bound to govern by established standing laws, promulgated and known to the people, and not by

> *"All this . . . to no other end but the peace, safety, and public good of the people."*

extemporary decrees; by indifferent [unbiased] and upright judges who are to decide controversies by these laws; and to employ the force of the community at home only in the execution of such laws, or abroad to prevent or redress foreign injuries, and secure the community from inroads and invasion. And all this to be directed to no other end but the peace, safety, and public good of the people.

—From John Locke, Two Treatises of Government, Thomas I. Cook, editor. New York: Free Press, 1947.

THINK ABOUT THIS

1. According to Locke, why do people unite to form societies and governments?
2. What do individuals give up when they live under a government, and what do they gain?

John Adams on Democratic Government

Another Enlightenment thinker, the French political writer Charles Louis de Secondat Montesquieu, claimed in an influential 1748 book called *L'Esprit des lois* (*The Spirit of the Law*) that a properly balanced government should consist of three branches: the legislative to make the laws, the executive to enforce them, and the judicial to uphold and interpret them. Each branch would check, or limit, the power of the others. Even before the federal Constitution of the United States embodied this system of checks and balances, Montesquieu's ideas had shaped the various state constitutions.

In 1787 John Adams, who had crafted the Massachusetts constitution, published *A Defence of the Constitutions of the United States,* which surveyed various forms of republican rule and argued that the state constitutions (especially that of Massachusetts) were models of good and balanced government.

John Adams spent the years 1785–1789 in England, serving as the U.S. ambassador. While Adams did not take part in the writing of the Constitution, he approved of the result because it separated the powers of government into three branches.

THERE CAN BE NO FREE government without a democratical branch in the government. Monarchies and aristocracies are in possession of the voice and influence of every university and academy in Europe. Democracy, simple democracy, never had a patron among men of letters. Democratical mixtures in government have lost almost all the advocates they ever had out of England and America. Men of letters must have a great deal of praise, and some of the necessaries, conveniences, and ornaments of life. Monarchies and aristocracies pay well and applaud liberally. The people have almost always expected to be served gratis, and to be paid for the honor of serving them; their applauses and adorations are bestowed too often on artifices and tricks, on hypocrisy and superstition, on flattery, bribes, and largesses. It is no wonder then that democracies and democratical mixtures are annihilated all over Europe, except on a

gratis
for free

largesses
gifts

John Adams was born in the house on the right, which still stands in Braintree, Massachusetts; it had belonged to the Adams family since the time of his great-grandfather. John and his wife, Abigail, later lived in the building on the left.

first pair
Adam and Eve

barren rock, a paltry fen, an inaccessible mountain, or an impenetrable forest. The people of England, to their immortal honor, are hitherto an exception; but, to the humiliation of human nature, they show very often that they are like other men. The people in America have now the best opportunity and greatest trust in their hands, that Providence ever committed to so small a number, since the transgression of the first pair; if they betray their trust, their guilt will merit even greater punishment than other nations have suffered, and the indignation of Heaven. If there is one certain truth to be collected from the history of all ages, it is this; that the people's rights and liberties, and the democratical mixture in a constitution, can never be preserved without a strong executive, or, in other words, without separating the executive from the legislative power. If the executive power, or any considerable part of it, is left in the hands either of an aristocratic or a democratical assembly, it will corrupt the legislature as necessarily as rust corrupts iron, or as arsenic poisons the human body; and when the legislature is corrupted, the people are undone.

—From *John Adams,* A Defence of the Constitutions of the United States, *in George W. Carey, editor,* The Political Writings of John Adams. *Washington, DC: Regnery, 2000. Originally published in 1786–1787.*

THINK ABOUT THIS

1. Why does Adams think that learned writers ("men of letters") do not generally support democracy?
2. Does this passage give you any insights into Adams's views on human nature?
3. What reason does Adams give for separating the executive from the legislative branch of government?

"Near to Perfection": Benjamin Franklin on the Constitution

At eighty-one years of age, Benjamin Franklin was the oldest delegate to the Constitutional Convention. He was also one of the most respected. People admired him for his intelligence, common sense, and ability to cut to the heart of an issue in a straightforward way. As the convention prepared to vote on the proposed Constitution, much disagreement remained about the plan of government it outlined.

Franklin offered his opinion, although, being in poor health, he had someone else read the speech for him. Even delivered in another's voice, the speech bore the unmistakable marks of Franklin's wit and plain language. Some historians believe that it swung the votes of enough delegates to result in the acceptance of the Constitution.

Printer, inventor, patriot, public servant, and diplomat, Benjamin Franklin (1706–1790) was one of the towering figures of early American life. This portrait was painted in 1782, during the nine years Franklin spent in France negotiating political and trade agreements for the United States.

I CONFESS THAT I DO NOT entirely approve of this Constitution at present; but, sir, I am not sure I shall never approve of it, for, having lived long, I have experienced many instances of being obliged, by better information or fuller consideration, to change opinions even on important subjects, which I once thought right, but found to be otherwise. It is therefore that, the older I grow, the more apt I am to doubt my own judgment of others. Most men, indeed, as well as most sects in religion, think themselves in possession of all truth, and that wherever others differ from them, it is so far error. Steele, a Protestant, in a dedication, tells the pope that the only difference between our two churches in their opinions of the certainty of their doctrine is, the Romish [Roman Catholic] Church is infallible, and the

King Louis XVI and Queen Marie Antoinette of France (seated) receive Franklin at the royal court. The American became tremendously popular with the French, who admired his wit, his learning, and his plain but gracious manners.

Church of England is never in the wrong. But, though many private persons think almost as highly of their own infallibility as of that of their sect, few express it so naturally as a certain French lady, who, in a little dispute with her sister, said: "But I meet with nobody but myself that is always in the right."

In these sentiments, sir, I agree to this Constitution with all its faults—if they are such—because I think a general government . . . may be a blessing to the people if well administered; and I believe, further, that this is likely to be well administered for a course of years, and can only end in despotism, as other forms have done before it, when the people shall become so corrupted as to need despotic government, being incapable of any other. I doubt, too, whether any other convention we can obtain may be able to make a better Constitution; for, when you assemble a

"It therefore astonishes me, sir, to find this system approaching so near to perfection."

number of men, to have the advantage of their joint wisdom, you inevitably assemble with those men all their prejudices, their passions, their errors of opinion, their local interests, and their selfish views. From such an assembly can a perfect production be expected?

It therefore astonishes me, sir, to find this system approaching so near to perfection as it does: and I think it will astonish our enemies, who are waiting with confidence to hear that our counsels are confounded.

—From Charles Hurd, editor, A Treasury of Great American Speeches. *New York: Hawthorn Books, 1959.*

THINK ABOUT THIS

1. What reasons does Franklin give for accepting the Constitution as written by the convention?
2. Under what circumstances does Franklin think democracy can turn into despotism?

"The American Nation and Its Homeland": From *The Federalist*

One of the *Federalist* authors was New York lawyer John Jay. Like other Federalists, he had a strong sense of nationalism—pride in the nation, belief that national unity outweighs other factors such as local or state interests, and devotion to national identity and goals. In the second *Federalist* paper, published during the debates over ratification of the Constitution, Jay urged readers to adopt a nationalist system of government rather than one that allowed the states to function independently.

IT HAS UNTIL LATELY BEEN a received and uncontradicted opinion that the prosperity of the people of America depended on their continuing firmly united, and the wishes, prayers, and efforts of our best and wisest citizens have been constantly directed to that object. But politicians now appear who insist that this opinion is erroneous, and that instead of looking for safety and happiness in union, we ought to seek it in a division of the States into distinct confederacies or sovereignties. . . .

It has often given me pleasure to observe that independent America was not com-

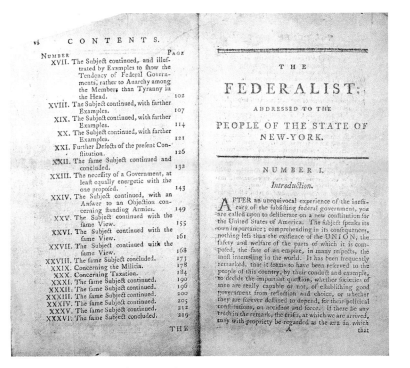

This first edition of *The Federalist* in book form appeared in 1788, as some states continued to debate whether or not to accept the Constitution. It argued the need for a strong central government.

posed of detached and distant territories, but that one connected, fertile, well-spreading country was the portion of our western sons of liberty. Providence has in a particular manner blessed it with a variety of soils and productions and watered it with innumerable streams for the delight and accommodation of its inhabitants. A succession of navigable waters forms a kind of chain round its borders, as if to knit it together; while the most noble rivers in the world, running at convenient distances, present them with highways for the easy communication of friendly aids and the mutual transportation and exchange of their various commodities.

With equal pleasure I have as often taken notice that Providence has been pleased to give this one connected country to one united people—a people descended from the same ancestors, speaking the same language, professing the same religion, attached to the same principles of government, very similar in their manners and customs, and who, by their joint counsels, arms, and efforts, fighting side by side throughout a long and bloody war, have nobly established their general liberty and independence.

> "This country and this people seem to have been made for each other."

This country and this people seem to have been made for each other, and it appears as if it was the design of Providence that an inheritance so proper and convenient for a band of brethren, united to each other by the strongest ties, should never be split into a number of unsocial, jealous, and alien sovereignties.

—From John Jay, The Federalist, *in Michael Lind, editor,* Hamilton's Republic. *New York: Free Press, 1997.*

THINK ABOUT THIS

1. How does Jay use geography to support nationalism? Do you agree with his argument?

2. Jay describes the population of the American colonies and the United States as "one united people." What evidence does he give that Americans are one people? Based on what you know about early America, do you think his statements are true?

An Anti-Federalist's Advice: Mercy Otis Warren Speaks to Future Americans

One of the strongest critics of the Constitution and of federalism was Mercy Otis Warren of Boston. She wrote and circulated a pamphlet outlining how the proposed federal government violated what she believed to be the basic principles of republicanism. Once the Bill of Rights had been added, however, she felt able to accept the Constitution. In her three-volume *History of the Rise, Progress, and Termination of the American Revolution,* published in 1805, Warren praised the Constitution, but she also warned future generations of Americans to be watchful and protective of their rights and liberties.

PERHAPS GENIUS HAS NEVER DEVISED a system more congenial to their wishes, or better adapted to the condition of man, than the American constitution. At the same time, it is left open to amendments whenever its imperfections are discovered by the wisdom of future generations, or when new contingencies may arise either at home or abroad, to make alterations necessary. On the principles of republicanism was this constitution founded; on these it may stand. Many corrections and amendments have already taken place, and it is at the present period as wise, as efficient, as respectable, as free, and we hope as permanent, as any constitution existing on earth.

—*From Mercy Otis Warren, in William Raymond Smith,* History as Argument.
The Hague, Netherlands: Mouton & Co., 1966.

LET NOT THE FRIVOLITY OF the domestic taste of the children of Columbia, . . . nor the examples of strangers of high or low degree . . . or the imposing attitude of distant nations, or the machinations of the bloody tyrants of Europe . . . rob them of their character, their morals, their religions, or their liberty. Any attempt, either by secret fraud, or open violence, to shake the union, to subvert the constitution, or undermine the just principles, which wrought out the American revolution, cannot be too severely censured. The principles of the revolution ought ever to be the pole-star of the statesman. It will be the wisdom, and probably the future effort of the American government, for ever to maintain . . . the

Mercy Otis Warren, an ardent supporter of the Revolution, had a lifelong interest in politics and government.

present neutral position of the United States. America may with propriety be styled a land of promise . . . a fair and fertile vineyard, which requires only the industrious care of the laborers to render it for a long time productive of the finest clusters in the full harvest of prosperity and freedom.

The people may again be reminded, that the elective franchise is in their own hands; that it ought not to be abused, either for personal gratifications, or the indulgence of partisan acrimony. They therefore cannot be too scrutinous on the character of their executive officers. No man should be lifted by the voice of his country to presidential rank, who may probably forget the republican designation, and sigh to wield a sceptre, instead of guarding sacredly the charter from the people.

sceptre
symbol of kingship or royal power

—*From Mercy Otis Warren, quoted in Jean Fritz,* Cast for a Revolution: Some American Friends and Enemies, 1728–1814. *Boston: Houghton Mifflin, 1972.*

THINK ABOUT THIS

1. What reasons does Warren give for amending, or changing, the Constitution?

2. Based on the second extract, what does Warren see as possible threats to Americans' freedoms?

Gilbert Stuart painted this portrait and more than a hundred other images of George Washington, the nation's first president. Three of Stuart's pictures can be considered primary sources because Washington posed for them, and the others are based on these three. One Stuart portrait of Washington is familiar to everyone—it appears on the American dollar bill.

Chapter 2

Presidents and Parties

DELEGATES TO THE Constitutional Convention had to answer the question of whether the United States should have a chief executive, a single person who would be the head of state. Some answered no, fearing that such an official would have powers too much like those of a king. They argued that the executive power should be shared by a small elected committee. Most delegates, however, felt that the government would work more efficiently with a single chief executive. In addition, they believed that the American people wanted a person, not a committee, to serve as the face and voice of their country.

The Constitution established the offices of the president, who would head the executive branch of government, and the vice president, who would replace the president if necessary. Both would be chosen by electors, individuals appointed by the legislatures of each state to vote for the presidential candidates favored by the citizens of that state. The candidate with the most electoral votes would become president, and the candidate with the second-highest number of votes would be vice president. The writers of the Constitution created this system, called the electoral college, because they feared that if citizens voted directly for their leaders, voters might be swayed by demagogues—ill-qualified candidates who played on their fear or greed. But if citizens' votes were filtered through the electoral college, they thought, the election process would be more likely to remain thoughtful and balanced. The electoral college was also an attempt to protect rural districts from being completely dominated in each election by the much more densely populated urban districts. A few members of the Constitutional Convention questioned whether the electoral college would accurately reflect the choices of the American people, and the question remains an issue in American politics today. Over the years, several presidents have been elected by the college even though they did not receive the greatest number of popular votes.

To no one's surprise, the first elected president was George Washington, the popular and respected Virginian who had led the American forces to victory in the Revolution. His vice president, John Adams, was elected the nation's second president when George Washington retired from office after eight years. By the time Adams was elected, however, something unforeseen had taken place in political life. The first parties, competing groups organized around different principles and leaders, had emerged. They formed along the split between Federalists and Anti-Federalists. One party became known as the Federalists, the other as the Republicans or Democratic-Republicans (not the same party as today's Republicans). Alexander Hamilton was the guiding spirit of the Federalists, who supported central government and tended to favor business interests. Thomas Jefferson and James Madison shaped the Republican position, which supported states' rights and was popular with workers and farmers.

The presidential election of 1796 was the first time that candidates had campaigned as representatives of parties, not simply as individuals. Because the electors voted for individuals, however, not parties, the election produced an awkward result: Adams, a Federalist, became president, but his vice president was Jefferson, the leading Republican. During the next presidential campaign, in 1800, each party presented a candidate for president and one for vice president. This time, however, a different problem arose. Jefferson was the Republican candidate for president. The Republicans also entered Aaron Burr into the election, expecting him to receive the second-highest number of votes and become vice president. But they each received the same number of electoral votes, which placed them in a tie for the presidency. Finally, after repeated voting by

Alexander Hamilton was one of the strongest voices of the Federalist Party. This portrait was painted in 1806, two years after Hamilton was killed by former vice president Aaron Burr in a duel that shocked the nation.

the House of Representatives, which was charged with selecting the winner, the tie broke. Jefferson became president, Burr vice president. (To prevent such deadlocks in the future, Congress promptly passed an amendment to the Constitution that required electors to vote separately for president and vice president.) Although the country's first two presidents had been Federalists, Republicans held the office for the rest of the New Republic era, under Jefferson, James Madison, James Monroe, and John Quincy Adams.

George Washington's Farewell Address to the People of the United States

When George Washington became the country's first president, there was no limit to the number of four-year terms a president could serve. Washington wanted to retire after his first term, but others persuaded him that the country needed him. Late in his second term, however, he decided firmly that he would not run for president again. On September 19, 1796, a Philadelphia newspaper called the *Daily American Advertiser* published a long essay by Washington that is known as his Farewell Address. Washington began the essay by explaining why he had decided to retire from office. After that, he spoke of the need for unity and a strong central government, and he gave his views on the course he thought the nation should follow. The following passage warns against political factions or parties, which Washington considered dangerous because they tended to divide, rather than to unite, the population.

THE ALTERNATE DOMINATION of one faction over another, sharpened by the spirit of revenge natural to a party dissension, which in different ages and countries has perpetrated the most horrid enormities, is itself a frightful despotism.—But this leads at length to a more formal and permanent despotism. The disorders and miseries which result, gradually incline the minds of men to seek security and repose in the absolute power of an individual; and, sooner or later, the chief of some prevailing faction, more able or more fortunate than his competitors, turns this disposition to the purpose of his own elevation on the ruins of public liberty.

Without looking forward to an extremity of this kind (which nevertheless ought not to be entirely out of sight) the common and continual mischiefs of the spirit of party are sufficient to make it the interest and duty of a wise people to discourage and restrain it.

It serves always to distract the public councils, and enfeeble the public administration. It agitates the community with ill founded jealousies and false alarms; kindles the animosity of one part against another; foments occasional riot and insurrection. It opens the door to foreign influence and corruption, which finds a facilitated access to the government itself through the channels of party passions. Thus the policy and the will of one country are subjected to the policy and will of another.

There is an opinion that parties in free countries are useful checks upon the administration of the government, and serve to keep alive the spirit of liberty. This within certain limits is probably true; and in governments of a monarchial cast, patriotism may look with indulgence, if not with favor, upon the spirit of party. But in those of

"The alternate domination of one faction over another . . . has perpetrated the most horrid enormities."

the popular character, in governments purely elective, it is a spirit not to be encouraged. From their natural tendency, it is certain there will always be enough of that spirit for every salutary purpose. And there being constant danger of excess, the effort ought to be, by force of public opinion, to mitigate and assuage vigilance to prevent it bursting into a flame, lest instead of warming, it should consume.

—*From George Washington,* Washington's Farewell Address to the People of the United States. *Washington, DC: WANT Publishing, 1985.*

THINK ABOUT THIS

1. According to Washington, what is the worst or most extreme evil caused by party politics? What are some of the lesser evils?
2. Why do you think Washington included this warning in his Farewell Address?
3. Can you imagine the United States today *without* political parties?

James Madison Outlines Republican Views

In 1791 Thomas Jefferson helped an editor named Philip Freneau start a newspaper called the *National Gazette.* The *Gazette* became a voice for the Republican Party, publishing many essays by Jefferson and Madison, although the authors did not always sign their names to their work (leading members of both parties frequently wrote anonymously in those days). On December 22, 1792, the *Gazette* published an essay titled "Who Are the Best Keepers of the People's Liberties?" In the article, Madison answered from the point of view of both the Republicans and their opponents, the Federalists, whom he calls Anti-Republicans.

Republican.—The people themselves. The sacred trust can be no where so safe as in the hands most interested in preserving it.

Anti-Republican.—The people are stupid, suspicious, licentious. They cannot safely trust themselves. When they have established government they should think of nothing but obedience, leaving the care of their liberties to their wiser rulers.

Republican.—Although men are born free, and all nations might be so, yet too true it is, that slavery has been the general lot of the human race. Ignorant—they have been cheated; asleep—they have been surprized; divided—the yoke has been forced upon them. But what is the lesson? That because the people *may* betray themselves, they ought to give themselves up, blindfold, to those who have an interest in betraying them? Rather conclude that the people ought to be enlightened, to be awakened, to be united, that after establishing a government they should watch over it, as well as obey it.

Anti-Republican.—You look at the surface only, where errors float, instead of fathoming the depths where truth lies hid. It is not the government that is disposed to fly off from the people: but the people that are ever ready to fly off from the government. Rather say then, enlighten the government, warn it to be vigilant, enrich it with influence, arm it with force, and to the people never pronounce but two words—*Submission* and *Confidence*.

Republican.—The centrifugal tendency then is in the people, not in the government, and the secret art lies in restraining the tendency, by augmenting the attractive principle of the government with all the

James Madison, shown here in his early thirties, became a leader of the Republican Party and the nation's fourth president.

weight that can be added to it. What a perversion of the natural order of things! to make *power* the primary and central object of the social system, and make *Liberty* but its satellite.

Anti-Republican.—The science of the stars can never instruct you in the mysteries of government. Wonderful as it may seem, the more you increase the attractive force of power, the more you enlarge the sphere of liberty; the more you make government independent and hostile towards the people, the better security you provide for their rights and interests. Hence the wisdom of the theory, which, after limiting the share of the people to a third of the government, and lessening the influence of that share by the mode and term of delegating it, establishes two grand hereditary orders, with feelings, habits, interests, and prerogatives all inverately hostile to the rights and interests of the people, yet by a mysterious operation all combining to fortify the people in both.

Republican.—Mysterious indeed! But mysteries belong to religion, not to government; to the ways of the Almighty, not to the works of man. And in religion itself there is nothing mysterious to its author; the mystery lies in the dimness of human sight. So in the institutions of man let there be no mystery, unless for those inferior beings endowed with a ray perhaps of the twilight vouchsafed to the first order of terrestrial creation.

Anti-Republican.—You are destitute, I perceive, of every quality of a good citizen, or rather of a good subject. You have neither the light of faith nor the spirit of obedience. I denounce you to the government as an accomplice of atheism and anarchy.

Republican.—And I forebear to denounce you to the people, though a blasphemer of their rights and an idolater of tyranny. Liberty disdains to persecute.

—From James Madison, quoted in Jack N. Rakove, editor, *James Madison: Writings. New York: Library Classics of the United States, 1999.*

1. How would you describe the Anti-Republican in Madison's essay?
2. Do you think it was possible for Madison to present the opposing point of view fairly?
3. What does Madison mean by "slavery has been the general lot of the human race"?

Alexander Hamilton's Letter about the Virginia and Kentucky Resolutions

Thomas Jefferson and James Madison sought to limit federal power through acts of the states. They wrote resolutions, or laws, that Virginia's state legislature enacted in 1798 and Kentucky's in 1799. These resolutions claimed that the states could decide for themselves whether federal laws were properly grounded in the Constitution. The Kentucky Resolutions went so far as to let the state overturn any federal law it found unconstitutional. The Federalists could not accept this challenge to central authority. Their foremost spokesperson, Alexander Hamilton, wrote to a Federalist senator named Theodore Sedgwick to rally opposition to the Virginia and Kentucky Resolutions.

New York Feby 2. 1799.

"This is a very serious business."

What, My Dear Sir, are you going to do with Virginia? This is a very serious business, which will call for all the wisdom and firmness of the Government. The following are the ideas which occur to me on the occasion.

The first thing in all great operations of such a Government

This 1884 picture shows a fiery young Alexander Hamilton, fist upraised, urging a Revolutionary-era crowd to seek liberty. Throughout his career, Hamilton won respect—even from political opponents—for his speechmaking skills.

as ours is to secure the opinion of the people. To this end, the proceedings of Virginia and Kentucke with the two laws complained of should be referred to a special Committee. That Committee should make a report exhibiting with great luminousness and particularity the reasons which support the constitutionality of those laws—the tendency of the doctrines advanced by Virginia and Kentucke to destroy the Constitution of the UStates—and, with calm dignity united with pathos, the full evidence which they afford of a regular conspiracy to overturn the government. And the Report should likewise dwell upon the inevitable effect and probably the intention of these proceedings to encourage a hostile foreign power to decline accommodation and proceed in hostility. The Government must [no]t merely [de]fend itself [bu]t must attack and arraign its enemies. But in all this, there should be great care to distinguish the people of Virginia from the legislature and even the greater part of those who may have concurred in the legislature from the Chiefs; manifesting indeed a strong confidence in the good sense and patriotism of the people, that they will not be the dupes of an insidious plan to disunite the people of America to break down their constitution & expose them to the enterprises of a foreign power. . . .

In the mean time the measures for raising the Military force should proceed with activity. Tis much to be lamented that so much delay has attended the execution of this measure. In times like the present not a moment ought to have been lost to secure the Government so powerful an auxiliary. . . . When a clever force has been collected let them be drawn toward Virginia for which there is an obvious pretext—& then let measures be taken to act upon the laws & put Virginia to the Test of resistance.

This plan will give time for the fervour of the moment to subside, for reason to resume the reins, and by dividing its enemies will enable the Government to triumph with ease. . . .

—*From Alexander Hamilton,* The Papers of Alexander Hamilton *(27 volumes),*
Harold Syrett, editor. New York: Columbia University Press, 1961–1987.
Quoted in Noble E. Cunningham, Jefferson vs. Hamilton: Confrontations
that Shaped a Nation. *New York: Bedford/St. Martin's, 2000.*

THINK ABOUT THIS

1. What does Hamilton fear will be the results of the Virginia and Kentucky Resolutions?
2. Outline Hamilton's plan, step by step, to defeat the resolutions.
3. How does his strategy, by playing on the fears and vanities of the people, make use of human psychology?
4. Do you think Hamilton was right to urge the government to use force against Virginia?

A Bid for Unity: Thomas Jefferson's First Inaugural Address

In his Farewell Address, Washington had warned of the problems caused by party politics. By the time Jefferson took office as president in March 1801, the nation's political life was dominated by the rivalry between the two parties, whose members frequently attacked one another in harsh, vicious terms. Although Jefferson had engaged in party politics as energetically as anyone, he made a speech at his inauguration in which he called for unity and an end to conflict. The "throes and convulsions," referred to in the second paragraph of the speech, is a reminder of the French Revolution of 1789, which Republicans had generally favored and Federalists had generally viewed as violent and uncontrolled.

Gilbert Stuart painted this portrait of Thomas Jefferson in 1805, midway through Jefferson's two terms as president. Historians consider it a highly accurate image—a valuable primary source from before the invention of photography.

DURING THE CONTEST of opinion through which we have passed, the animation of discussions and of exertions has sometimes worn an aspect which might impose on strangers unused to think freely, and to speak and to write what they think; but this being now decided by the voice of the nation, announced according to the rules of the Constitution, all will of course arrange themselves under the will of the law, and unite in common efforts for the common good. All too will bear in mind this sacred principle, that though the will of the majority is in all cases to prevail, that will, to be rightful, must be reasonable; that the minority possess their equal rights, which equal laws must protect, and to violate which would be oppression.

Let us then, fellow-citizens, unite with one heart and one mind, let us restore to social intercourse that harmony and affection without which liberty and even life itself are but dreary things. And let us reflect, that having banished from our land that religious intolerance under which mankind so long bled and suffered, we have yet gained little, if we countenance a political intolerance, as despotic, as wicked, and as capable of as bitter and bloody persecutions. During the throes and convulsions of the ancient world, during the agonizing spasms of infuriated man, seeking through blood and slaughter his long-lost liberty, it was not wonderful that the agitation of the billows should reach even this distant and peaceful shore; that this should be more felt and feared by some, and less by others, and should divide opinions as to measures of safety; but every difference of opinion is not a difference of principle. We have called by different names brethren of the same principle. We are all Republicans; we are all Federalists.

"We are all Republicans; we are all Federalists."

THE PRESENT State of our COUNTRY.

George Washington, who had warned of the evils of political parties, watches worriedly as representatives of the two main parties try to topple the pillars that support "Peace and Plenty, Liberty and Independence." They also support the words "United we stand, Divided we fall."

If there be any among us who wish to dissolve this Union, or to change its republican form, let them stand undisturbed as monuments of the safety with which error of opinion may be tolerated, where reason is left free to combat it. I know, indeed, that some honest men fear that a republican government cannot be strong; that this government is not strong enough. But would the honest patriot, in the full tide of successful experiment, abandon a government which has so far kept us free and firm, on the theoretic and visionary fear, that this government, the world's best hope, may, by possibility, want energy to preserve itself? I trust not. I believe this, on the contrary, the strongest government on earth. I believe it the only one where every man, at the call of the law, would fly to the standard of the law, and would meet invasions of the public order as his own personal concern. Sometimes it is said that man cannot be trusted with the government of himself. Can he then be trusted with the government of others? Or, have we found angels in the form of kings, to govern him? Let history answer this question.

Let us then, with courage and confidence, pursue our own federal and republican principles; our attachment to union and representative government. Kindly separated by nature and a wide ocean from the exterminating havoc of one quarter of the globe; too high-minded to endure the degradation of the others, possessing a chosen country, with room enough for our descendants to the thousandth and thousandth generation, entertaining a due sense of our equal right to the use of our own faculties, to the acquisition of our own industry, to honor and confidence from our fellow-citizens, resulting not from birth, but from our actions and their sense of them, enlightened by a benign religion, professed in deed and practised in various forms, yet all of them inculcating honesty, truth, temperance, gratitude, and love of man, acknowledging and adoring an overruling Providence, which, by all its dispensations, proves that it delights in the happiness of man here, and his greater happiness hereafter; with all these blessings, what more is necessary to make us a happy and prosperous people? Still one thing more, fellow-citizens, a wise and frugal government, which shall restrain men from injuring one another, shall leave them otherwise free to regulate their own pursuits of industry and improvement, and shall not take from the mouth of labor the bread it has earned. This is the sum of good government; and this is necessary to close the circle of our felicities.

—From Thomas Jefferson, First Inaugural Address, quoted in Charles Hurd, editor, Great American Speeches. *New York: Hawthorn Books, 1959.*

THINK ABOUT THIS

1. What reasons might Jefferson have had for urging unity and an end to party conflict?
2. What does he mean by the statement "We are all Republicans; we are all Federalists"?
3. Does Jefferson define good government by what it does or by what it does not do?

Edward Everett on the Deaths of Adams and Jefferson

John Adams and Thomas Jefferson, fellow Patriots during the Revolution, had become bitter political rivals afterward. Aside from George Washington, no one left a greater mark on the early years of the United States than Adams and Jefferson, each of whom served as vice president and president. Later in their lives, long after they retired from politics, the two men left their political differences behind and exchanged many friendly letters. They realized that they were among the last surviving founders of the United States, a link that was broken when both men died on the same day: July 4, 1826. Less than a month later, a diplomat, politician, and scholar named Edward Everett, one of the best known American speech-makers of the nineteenth century, delivered a speech in their honor.

THE JUBILEE OF AMERICA is turned into mourning. Its joy is mingled with sadness; its silver trumpet breathes a mingled strain. Henceforward, while America exists among the nations of the earth, the first emotion of the Fourth of July will be of joy and triumph in the great event which immortalizes the day; the second will be one of chastened and tender recollection of the venerable men who departed on the morning of the jubilee. This mingled emotion of

Another of John Lewis Krimmel's patriotic scenes of public life in the early republic. This one shows the people of Philadelphia celebrating the Fourth of July, 1819.

triumph and sadness has sealed the beauty and sublimity of our great anniversary. . . .

Friends, fellow citizens, free, prosperous, happy Americans! The men who did so much to make you so are no more. The men who gave nothing to pleasure in youth, nothing to repose in age, but all to that country, whose beloved name filled their hearts, as it does ours, with joy, can now do no more for us; nor we for them. But their memory remains, we will cherish it; their bright example remains, we will strive to imitate it; the fruit of their wise counsels and noble acts remains, we will gratefully enjoy it. . . .

" . . . the fruit of their wise counsels and noble acts remains."

The contemporary and successive generations of men will disappear, and in the long lapse of ages, the races of America, like those of Greece and Rome, may pass away. The fabric of American freedom, like all things human, however firm and fair, may crumble into dust. But the cause in which these our fathers shone is immortal. They did that to which no age, no people of civilized men, can be indifferent. Their eulogy will be uttered in other languages, when those we speak, like us who speak them, shall be all forgotten. And when the great account of humanity shall be closed, in the bright list of those who have best adorned and served it, shall be found the names of our Adams and our Jefferson!

—*From Edward Everett, quoted in Charles Hurd, editor,* Great American Speeches. *New York: Hawthorn Books, 1959.*

THINK ABOUT THIS

1. Why do you think Everett compared the United States with Greece and Rome?

2. What achievement of Adams and Jefferson does Everett believe future peoples will remember and admire?

Chapter 3

International Affairs

NO SOONER HAD THE UNITED STATES come into existence than it had to deal with other countries. Some of the people who had fought for independence and helped form the young nation's government also acted as diplomats, charged with the often delicate task of making deals, resolving problems, and sealing alliances with other countries. Benjamin Franklin, John Adams, and Thomas Jefferson all represented the United States on the world stage at various times.

Relations with other countries revolved around many issues. Trade was a frequent problem. Great Britain and France were at war during the early years of the American republic, and each nation tried to prevent the United States from trading with its enemy. The British attacked American ships that they thought were trading with France, and France prepared to attack U.S. vessels that engaged in trade with Britain. In 1807 President Thomas Jefferson tried to solve this problem by making it illegal for Americans to trade with *any* foreign country. But his trade

During the War of 1812, British forces attacked Fort McHenry in the harbor of Baltimore, Maryland. The attack failed to bring down the fort's U.S. flag, inspiring a young attorney named Francis Scott Key to write "The Star-Spangled Banner." The song became the American anthem—a key piece of national identity with roots in the New Republic period.

embargo, as it was called, was a disaster for the U.S. economy and was soon cancelled.

Many conflicts between the United States and Great Britain stemmed from the Revolutionary War. The British deeply resented their defeat and the loss of their colonies, and for a time they maintained army forts on U.S. territory in the Ohio River valley. They also engaged in a practice called impressment, forcing men to serve in their navy. British naval vessels stopped U.S. ships at sea and examined the crew. Anyone suspected of being a deserter from the British navy was seized, taken into service, and often harshly punished. Some sailors on U.S. ships *were* British deserters, but other victims of impressment were simply unlucky Americans, and their fate infuriated the American public. Impressment was one of the causes of a war that broke out in 1812 between the United States and Great Britain. Once again the British failed to overcome the Americans. The end of the War of 1812 left the United States not only victorious but also confident. America's leaders felt sure of their country's strength and of its ability to take a major role in world affairs.

War in the Northwest Territory: A British Officer on the American Frontier

In the 1783 Treaty of Paris that ended the Revolutionary War, Great Britain had agreed to abandon its forts in the Ohio River valley, which had become part of the United States. They did not keep this agreement, and for some years officers and soldiers from British Canada remained stationed in what Americans now called their Northwest Territory. American settlers in the area accused the British of encouraging the local Native Americans to attack U.S. settlers and of supplying attackers with guns and ammunition. Sometimes, however, the British saved American lives, as in a June 1788 episode recorded in the diary of Thomas Hughes, a British officer at Fort Detroit.

THE INDIANS, HAVING TAKEN UP the hatchet against the Americans, took a number of prisoners on the Ohio—most of whom they burnt as a sacrifice to the manes of their friends who were killed at the Shawnees' towns in the fall of 1786; some prisoners were however lucky enough to be brought to Detroit, and by the interest of Captain McKee with the savages restored to their liberty, amongst the rest a Mr. Ridout. He was a merchant—had been collecting debts in the back countries and was on his way to New Orleans, with what he had been able to scrape together. In going down the Ohio they were surprised at seeing a large boat near the shore, where they knew there could be no inhabitants. When they came near about forty Indians jumpt into her, and made after them; resistance being hopeless they surrendered—every thing was in an instant plundered, and Mr. Ridout and his crew stript. When they landed they found the savage party consisted of 90 warriors of different nations; they had taken a boat the day before and had in all ten prisoners. . . . The next day the plunder &c was to be divided—each nation separated, and made their own fire—an old Indian gave to each party its portion of the booty, and all appeared contented. They then came to the prisoners. The first was given to a Cherokee who took him a little on

"The Indians . . . took a number of prisoners on the Ohio."

Detroit as it appeared in the early 1790s. Although on U.S. soil, the fort and settlement remained in British hands until 1796.

one side and tomahawked him—and 2nd and 3rd as soon as taken out had belts of black wampum put round their necks and were carried away—the fourth was given to four young Cherokees who put him in the middle of them, and shook rattles made of deers' sinews around him, and then turning to the woods seemed to make some incantations. This made the prisoner very uneasy; he was a Mr. Richardson, who it was imagined had been guilty of some crimes and was running from justice.

—From A Journal by Thomas Hughes, *E. A. Benians, editor.*
Cambridge, England: Cambridge University Press, 1947.

Curses on the "Arch Traitor": Americans Respond to the Jay Treaty

In 1794 the United States sent John Jay, a former secretary of foreign affairs and current chief justice of the Supreme Court, to London to make a trade agreement with Great Britain. Jay negotiated an agreement known as the Jay Treaty. The treaty smoothed over several points of dispute between the United States and Britain, but American citizens were outraged because it did not require the British to end such hated practices as impressing U.S. sailors and seizing French goods from U.S. ships. Congress barely approved the treaty. Many Americans, feeling that Jay had given in to British interests, regarded him as a traitor. To show their outrage, citizens in several cities destroyed effigies—crude figures—of him. Jay hoped to become the country's second president, but the unpopular treaty probably ruined his chance. The following newspaper accounts reflect how high public feeling was running against the treaty-maker.

[A] NUMBER OF RESPECTABLE CITIZENS, of this place and its vicinity, on Saturday last, ordered a likeness of this evil genius of western America to be made, which was soon well executed. At the appointed hour, he was ushered forth from a barber's shop, amidst the shouts of the

Americans did not hesitate to show their disapproval of government policies. Angry mobs burned images of John Jay after he made an unpopular treaty with Great Britain.

people, . . . and placed erect on the platform of the pillory. . . . After exhibiting him in this condition for some time, he was ordered to be guillotined, which was soon dexterously executed, and a flame instantly applied to him, which finding its way to a quantity of powder, which was lodged in his body, produced such an explosion that after it there was scarcely to be found a particle of the [effigy].—*New York Journal,* August 2, 1794.

At Philadelphia, on the 4th of July (the anniversary of the *glorious* independence), Mr. Jay and the Senate were burnt in effigy. . . . The figure of John Jay . . . [held] in his right hand a pair of scales, containing in one scale American Liberty and Independence . . . in the other, British gold. . . . From the mouth of the figure issued these words, "Come up to my price, and I will sell you my country." The figure was burned at Kensington amid the acclamations of hundreds of citizens. —Philadelphia *Democratic Printer,* July 4, 1795.

Notice is hereby given, that *in case the treaty entered into by that d——-n'd Arch Traitor, J——n J-y, with the British tyrant should be ratified,* a petition will be presented to the next General Assembly of Virginia at their next session praying that the said state *may recede from the Union,* and be left under the government and protection of One Hundred Thousand Free and Independent Virginians.—Richmond *Notice,* July 31, 1795.

—*From Robert Rankin,* University of California Chronicle: An Official Record *(Vol. IX, No. 2, Supplement). Berkeley, CA: University Press, 1907.*

THINK ABOUT THIS

Why do you think Americans were so angry that the treaty did not contain all the terms they had wanted?

War against the Barbary Pirates

The American shipping industry grew rapidly in the years of the new republic, but American vessels ran into trouble in the Mediterranean Sea. The coast of North Africa, known as the Barbary Coast, was the stronghold of pirates who seized the ships of any nation that did not pay them for safe passage. In 1801 the United States refused to increase its payments to the Barbary state of Tripoli. A few years later, the pirates of Tripoli, whom the Americans called Turks, captured an American warship, the *Philadelphia.* A young naval officer named Stephen Decatur became a hero by leading an attack force into Tripoli's harbor, fighting his way to the *Philadelphia,* boarding it, and burning it so that it could not be turned into a pirate ship. Later Decatur took part in an attack on the pirates' gunboats, or small warships. Decatur described the battle of the gunboats in a letter to a friend and fellow officer.

I FOUND THAT HAND-TO-HAND is not child's play—'tis kill or be killed. You no doubt recollect the conversation which we had when in the city of Washington. I then informed you that it was my intention to board if ever I had an opportunity, and that it was my opinion there could be no doubt of the issue. You will not doubt me, I hope, when I say that I am glad the event has proved my ideas were correct. I always thought we could lick them their own way and give them two to one. The first boat, they were thirty-six to

" . . . 'tis kill or be killed. "

Stephen Decatur of the U.S. Navy became a hero after he burned the American ship *Philadelphia* to keep it from becoming a pirate vessel.

twenty; we carried it without much fuss. The second was twenty-four to ten; they also went to the leeward. I had eighteen Italians in the boat with me, who claim the honor of the day. While we were fighting, they prayed. They are convinced we could not have been so fortunate unless their prayers had been heard. This might have been the case; therefore we could not contradict it. Some of the Turks died like men, but much the greater died like women.

—*From* Naval Documents Related to the United States Wars with the Barbary Powers. *Washington, DC: Office of Naval Records, 1934–1944. Quoted in Glenn Tucker,* Dawn Like Thunder: The Barbary Wars and the Birth of the U.S. Navy. *Indianapolis, IN: Bobbs-Merrill, 1963.*

THINK ABOUT THIS

1. Based on this passage, what do you think was Decatur's attitude toward his opponents?
2. What do you think was the purpose of Decatur's letter to his friend?

An American Victory at Sea: The *Constitution* vs. the *Guerrière*

The United States Navy performed exceptionally well in the War of 1812, winning a number of important battles. These victories not only gave the U.S. military advantages by destroying or capturing enemy ships, but they also boosted Americans' morale and gave them something to cheer about. One of the most thrilling victories was that of the U.S. frigate *Constitution* against the British *Guerrière*. American citizen William B. Orne later described the event from an unusual point of view: He was aboard the *Guerrière*, which had earlier captured his merchant ship.

frigate
warship

AT TWO P.M. WE DISCOVERED a large sail to windward bearing about north from us. We soon made her out to be a frigate. She was steering off from the wind, with her head to the southwest, evidently with the intention of cutting us off as soon as possible. Signals were soon made by the *Guerrière,* but as they were not answered the conclusion was, of course, that she was either a French or American frigate. Captain Dacres appeared anxious to ascertain her character and after looking at her for that purpose, handed me his spy-glass, requesting me to give him my opinion of the stranger. I soon saw from the peculiarity of her sails and from her general appearance that she was, without doubt, an American frigate, and communicated the same to Captain Dacres. He immediately replied that he thought she came down too boldly for an American, but soon after added, "The better he behaves, the more honor we shall gain by taking him."

When the strange frigate came down to within two or three miles' distance, he hauled upon the wind, took in all his light sails, reefed his topsails, and deliberately prepared for action. It was now about five o'clock in the afternoon when he filled away and ran down for the *Guerrière.* At this moment Captain Dacres politely said to me: "Captain Orne, as I suppose you do not wish to fight against your own countrymen, you are at liberty to go below the water-line." It was not long after this before I retired from the quarter-deck to the cock-pit; of course I saw no more of the action until the firing ceased, but I heard and felt much of its effects; for soon after I left the deck the firing commenced on board the *Guerrière,* and was kept up almost incessantly until about six o'clock when I heard a tremendous explosion from the opposing frigate. The effect of her shot seemed to make the *Guerrière* reel and tremble as though she had received the shock of an earthquake.

Immediately after this, I heard a tremendous crash on deck and was told that the mizzen-mast was shot away. In a few moments afterward, the cock-pit was filled with wounded men. After the firing

had ceased I went on deck and there beheld a scene which it would be difficult to describe: all the *Guerrière*'s masts were shot away and, as she had no sails to steady her, she lay rolling like a log in the trough of the sea. Many of the men were employed in throwing the dead overboard. The decks had the appearance of a butcher's slaughterhouse; the gun tackles were not made fast and several of the guns got loose and were surging from one side to the other.

The 1812 sea battle between the American *Constitution* and the British *Guerrière*. The U.S. ship was nicknamed *Old Ironsides* after a sailor saw a cannonball bounce off its hull.

Some of the petty officers and seamen, after the action, got liquor and were intoxicated; and what with the groans of the wounded, the noise and confusion of the enraged survivors of the ill-fated ship rendered the whole scene a perfect hell.

—*From William B. Orne, quoted in Ralph D. Paine,* The Fight for a Free Sea: A Chronicle of the War of 1812. *New Haven, CT: Yale University Press, 1920.*

1. How would you describe the relationship between the British captain (Dacres) and his American prisoner?
2. Does it seem like an appropriate attitude between enemies? Why or why not?

Policing the Americas: The Monroe Doctrine

During the early nineteenth century, wars of independence broke out in Central and South America, and some Spanish colonies declared themselves free nations. Spain asked France, Austria, Russia, and Germany for help in regaining control of its former possessions. Because the United States did not want the European powers active in the Americas, President James Monroe made a speech in 1823 expressing what would come to be called the Monroe Doctrine. Crafted by secretary of state John Quincy Adams, the Monroe Doctrine said that the United States would leave existing colonies alone but would resist efforts by Europeans to establish any new colonies in the Americas.

[T]HE OCCASION HAS BEEN JUDGED proper, for asserting as a principle in which the rights and interests of the United States are involved, that the American Continents, by the free and independent condition which they have assumed and maintain, are henceforth not to be considered as subjects for future colonization by any European Power. . . . In the wars of the European powers, in matters relating to themselves, we have never taken any part, nor does it comport with our policy, so to do. It is only when our rights are invaded, or seriously menaced, that we resent injuries, or make preparation for our defense. With the movements in this Hemisphere we are of necessity

President James Monroe (standing) and his advisers discuss the Monroe Doctrine, which warned the nations of Europe not to interfere in the politics of the Americas.

more immediately connected, and by causes which must be obvious to all enlightened and impartial observers. . . . We owe it therefore to candor, and to the amicable relations existing between the United States and those powers, to declare that we should consider any attempt on their part to extend their system to any portions of this Hemisphere, as dangerous to our peace and safety. With the existing Colonies or dependencies of any European power, we have not interfered, and shall not interfere. But with the Governments who have declared their Independence, and maintained it, and whose Independence we have, on great consideration, and on just principles acknowledged, we could not view any interposition for the purpose of oppressing them, or controlling in any other manner, their destiny, by any European power, in any other light, than as the manifestation of an unfriendly disposition toward the United States.

—From James Monroe, quoted in George Dangerfield, The Era of Good Feelings. New York: Harcourt, Brace & World, 1952.

THINK ABOUT THIS

1. Monroe argued that what happens throughout the Americas is of concern to the United States? Do you agree with the Monroe Doctrine?

2. How do you think other countries in the Americas feel about the Monroe Doctrine?

The president's mansion was part of the grand new national capital rising in Washington, DC. A fire set by the British during the War of 1812 darkened its stone walls with soot, so afterward it was painted white. People began calling the mansion "the white house," and the name became official in 1901.

Chapter 4

American Affairs

SOME OF THE WORST PROBLEMS facing the brand-new United States were money problems. Great Britain would no longer let American merchants sell goods to Caribbean islands under British control, which had been an important market for American agricultural products and timber. As a result, farmers, merchants, and others across the United States saw their incomes shrink. At the same time, the state governments, desperate to raise money, were raising taxes. Farmers, shopkeepers, and others who could not pay their taxes saw their property seized by state officials. Their resentment was so great that some of them, led by a former army officer named Daniel Shays, started an armed rebellion in Massachusetts in 1786. The local militia soon crushed the uprising, but it had made some Americans wonder whether their new country could remain stable. Would those who had refused to be governed by Great Britain submit to an American government, or would citizens rebel whenever things got difficult? Over time, as the powers of the federal government increased, the chance of a serious revolt against authority decreased.

Another matter of national concern was the location of a new, permanent national capital. Both New York City and Philadelphia had served as centers of government, but as early as 1783 the Continental Congress had agreed to choose a new place to meet. Regions and cities competed to claim the capital, but the final choice came about as the result of a political deal. Alexander Hamilton needed the support of the southern states for his plan to have the federal government pay the states' debts. In return for their support, he used his influence to ensure that the national capital would be located in the south. The capital city would contain the Capitol, the building where Congress would meet.

No event was more significant to the early republic than the Louisiana Purchase of 1803, in which President Thomas Jefferson bought the Louisiana Territory from France. Overnight, the size of the United States doubled, and the vast territory between the Mississippi River and the Rocky Mountains was open to American exploration and use. Jefferson sent an expedition headed by army officers Meriwether Lewis and William Clark to investigate the country's new territory. They also crossed the land beyond the Rockies, all the way to the Pacific Ocean—territory that did not belong to the United States but, Jefferson hoped, one day would. The Lewis and Clark expedition is a good symbol for the United States in the early decades of the nineteenth century: ambitious, practical, successful, and looking toward the future.

A New Capital City: Thomas Jefferson on the Creation of Washington, DC

Thomas Jefferson was deeply involved in the planning of the new national capital city, Washington, DC, which was to be built on empty land along the Potomac River between Maryland and Virginia. Jefferson had always been interested in architecture and city planning, and he had made a careful study of the layout and buildings of many European cities. In letters to Pierre Charles L'Enfant, the architect hired by President Washington to design the capital, Jefferson offered a steady stream of suggestions along with the official decisions of the federal commission in charge of the project.

Sir:

I am favored with your letter of the 4 instant, and in complyance with your request I have examined my papers and found the plans of Frankfort on the Mayne, Carlsruhe, Amsterdam, Strasburg, Paris, Orleans, Bordeaux, Lyons, Montpelier, Marseilles, Turin, and Milan, which I send in a roll by this Post. They are on large and accurate scales, having been procured by me while in those respective cities myself. As they are connected with the notes I made in my travels, and often necessary to explain them to myself, I will beg your care of them and to return them when no longer useful to you, leaving you absolutely free to keep them as long as useful. I am happy that the President has left the planning of the Town in such good hands, and have no doubt it will be done to general satisfaction. . . . Having communicated to the President, before he went away, such general ideas on the subject of the Town, as occurred to me, I make no doubt that, in explaining himself to you on the subject, he has interwoven with his own ideas, such of mine as he approved. . . . Whenever it is

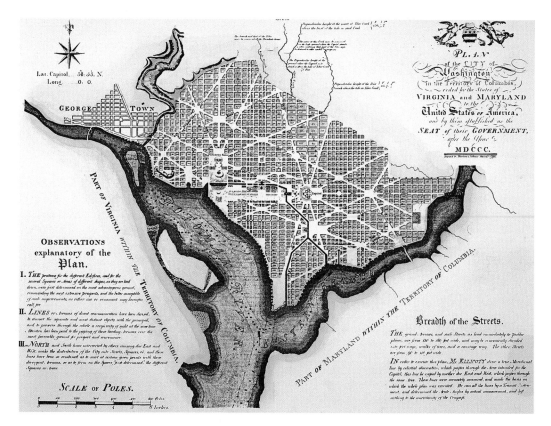

A map made in 1792 shows the elegant design of the capital city, nestled between two rivers, with grids of streets broken up by diagonal avenues and plazas.

proposed to prepare plans for the Capitol, I should prefer the adoption of some one of the models of antiquity [ancient Greece and Rome], which have had the approbation of thousands of years, and for the President's House I should prefer the celebrated fronts of modern buildings, which have already received the approbation of all good judges. Such are the Galerie du Louvre, the Gardes meubles, and two fronts of the Hotel de Salm. But of this it is yet time enough to consider, in the mean time I am with great esteem Sir &c. [April 10, 1791]

Sir:

We have agreed that the federal District will be called "The Territory of Columbia," and the federal City "The City of Washington": the title of the map will, therefore, be "A Map of the City of Washington in the Territory of Columbia."

We have also agreed the streets be named alphabetically one way, and numerically the other; the former divided into North and South letters, the latter into East and West numbers from the Capitol. Maj. Ellicott, with proper asistance, will immediately take and soon furnish you with soundings of the [river] to be inserted in the map. We expect he will also furnish you with the direction of a proposed post road which we wish to have noticed in the map.

We request you to inquire for L'Brunt, the brickmaker, of whom you had a memorandum; and, if he is carrying on his business, it will be well for you to see his bricks before you converse with him on the subject of his removal next Spring; if you approve his bricks, to inquire whether we could have him and on what terms.

[September 9, 1791]

—*From* The Writings of Thomas Jefferson and Proceedings of the Commissioners, *National Archives. Quoted in Saul K. Padover, editor,* Thomas Jefferson and the National Capital. *Washington, DC: U.S. Government Printing Office, 1946.*

THINK ABOUT THIS

1. Why do you think Jefferson wanted L'Enfant to use European cities and buildings modeled on ancient Rome and Greece as guides?

2. What reasons can you suggest for the system of identifying Washington's streets?

A Threat to Freedom of the Press: The Alien and Sedition Acts

The Jay Treaty of 1794 between the United States and Great Britain did more than make John Jay unpopular at home. It also angered the French, who viewed it as too favorable to their British enemies.

French and American ships clashed at sea during the late 1790s, although the two nations never formally declared war. In 1798 Congess, fearing that Europeans living in the United States might betray the United States in the event of war, passed laws called the Alien and Sedition Acts. The Sedition Act, which made it illegal to publish criticism of the government, came under attack as a violation of the First Amendment to the Constitution, which guarantees freedom of the press. John Nicholas of Virginia spoke out against the Sedition Act in the House of Representatives in 1799.

THE LAW HAS BEEN CURRENT by the fair pretence of punishing nothing but falsehood, and by holding out to the accused the liberty of proving the truth of the writing; but it was from the first apprehended and it seems now to be adjudged (the doctrine has certainly been asserted on this floor), that matters of opinion, arising on notorious facts, come under the law. If this is the case, where is the advantage of the law requiring that the writing should be false before a man shall be liable to punishment, or of his having the liberty of proving the truth of his writing? Of the truth of facts there is an almost certain test; the belief of honest men is certain enough to entitle it to great confidence; but their opinions have no certainty at all. The trial of the truth of opinions, in the best state of society, would be altogether precarious, and perhaps a jury of twelve men never could be found to agree in any one opinion. At the present moment, when, unfortunately, opinion is almost entirely governed by prejudice and passion, it may be more decided, but nobody will say it is more respectable. Chance must determine whether political opinions are true or false, and it will not unfrequently happen that a man will be punished for publishing opinions which are sincerely his, and which are of a nature to be extremely interesting to the public, merely because accident or design has collected a jury of different sentiments.

. . . . Upon the whole, therefore, I am fully satisfied that no power is given by the Constitution to control the press, and that such laws are expressly prohibited by the amendment. I think it inconsistent with the nature of our Government that its administration should have power to restrain animadversions on public measures.

animadversions
criticisms or negative statements

—From John Nicholas, speech before the House of Representatives, quoted in Alexander Johnson, editor, American Orations. *New York: G. P. Putnam's Sons, 1896.*

THINK ABOUT THIS

1. Why does Nicholas highlight the difference between fact and opinion?
2. Do you agree that people should have the freedom to publish any and all opinions? Can you think of instances in which this right should be curtailed? If so, how would you justify limiting the right of free speech?

Lewis and Clark Explore the West: Letter to the Oto Indians

During their journey across the West, Meriwether Lewis and William Clark gathered much information about geography, wildlife, and natural resources, as President Jefferson had requested. Acting on another of Jefferson's orders, they also delivered messages to the Native American groups they encountered in the Louisiana Territory. The explorers' job was to notify these groups that the region no longer belonged to its old masters, Spain and France, but had passed into the control of the United States. Lewis and Clark greeted the Indians in the name of the president, whom the explorers described as "the great Chief of the Seventeen great nations of America" (the seventeen states).

Children:—Commissioned and sent by the great Chief of the Seventeen great nations of America, we have come to inform you, as we go also to inform all the nations of red men who inhabit the borders of the Missouri, that a great council was lately held between this great Chief of the Seventeen great nations of America, and your old fathers the french and Spaniards; and that in this great council it was agreed that all the white men of Louisiana, inhabiting the waters of the Missouri and Mississippi should obey the commands of this great chief; he has accordingly adopted them as his children and they now form one common family with us: your old traders are of this description; they are no longer the

Future president James Monroe (*right*) signs the Louisiana Purchase in Paris on April 30, 1803. History's best real-estate deal, the purchase doubled the size of the United States for a bargain price.

Subjects of France or Spain, but have become the Citizens of the Seventeen great nations of america, and are bound to obey the commands of their great Chief the President who is now your only great father:—

. . . . *Children:*—From what has been said, you will readily perceive, that the great chief of the Seventeen great nations of America, has become your only father; he is the only friend to whom you can now look for protection, or from whom you can ask favours, or receive good councils, and he will take care that you shall have no just cause to regret this change; he will serve you, & not deceive you.

. . . . *Children:*—Know that this great chief, as powerfull as he is just, and as beneficent as he is wise, always entertaining a Sincere and friendly disposition towards the red people of America, has commanded us his war chiefs to undertake this long journey, which we have so far accomplished with great labour & much expence, in order to council with yourselves and his other red-children on the troubled waters, to give you his good advice; to point out to you the road in which you must walk to obtain happiness. He has further commanded us to tell you that when you accept his flag and medal, you accept therewith his hand of friendship, which will never be withdrawn from your nation as long as you continue to follow the councils which he may command his chiefs to give you, and shut your ears to the councils of Bad birds.

—From Lewis and Clark's *Letter to the Oto Indians. Quoted in* Letters of a Nation, *Andrew Carroll, editor. New York: Kodansha International, 1997.*

THINK ABOUT THIS

1. Why were the Indians addressed as "children"?
2. Why do you think Lewis and Clark emphasized the claim that the president was now the Indians' "only father" and "only friend"?
3. What might they have meant by the reference to "Bad birds"?

"The Dangers of American Liberty"

The United States was a democracy, but it was not a classless society. Despite the new nation's emphasis on equal rights and equal treatment under the law, deep divisions remained between upper-class, educated Americans and the less polished laborers and backwoodsmen who made up the lower class. Some members of the elite class felt little kinship with the masses. They feared that America's experiment in democracy would decay into rule by demagogues, politicians who appealed to the emotions of ignorant mobs. Fisher Ames, a Federalist from Boston, expressed this point of view in an essay written in 1805.

THE PEOPLE, AS A WHOLE, cannot deliberate. Nevertheless, they will feel an irresistible impulse to act, and their resolutions will be dictated to them by their demagogues. The consciousness, or the opinion, that they possess the supreme power, will inspire inordinate passions; and the violent men, who are the most forward to gratify those passions, will be their favourites. What is called the government of the people is in fact too often the arbitrary power of such men. Here, then, we have the faithful portrait of democracy. What avails the boasted *power* of individual citizens? or of what value is the will of the majority, if that will is dictated by a committee of demagogues, and law and right are in fact at the mercy of a victorious faction? To make a nation free, the crafty must be kept in awe, and the violent in restraint. The weak and the simple find their liberty arise not from their own individual sovereignty, but from the power of law and justice over all. It is only by the due restraint of others, that I am free.

   . . . The truth is, and let it humble our pride, the most ferocious of all animals, when his passions are roused to fury and are uncontrolled, is man; and of all governments, the worst is that which never fails to excite, but was never found to restrain those passions, that is, democracy. It is an illuminated hell, that in the midst of remorse, horrour, and torture, rings with festivity; for experience shews, that one joy remains to this most malignant description of the damned, the power to make others wretched. When a man looks round and sees his neighbours mild and merciful, he cannot feel afraid of the abuse of their power over him; and surely if they oppress me, he will say, they will spare their own liberty, for that is dear to all mankind. It is so. The human heart is so constituted that a man loves liberty as naturally as himself. Yet liberty is a rare thing in the world, though the love of it is so universal. . . .

" . . . liberty is a rare thing in the world."

—From Fisher Ames, "The Dangers of Liberty," quoted in Howard Mumford Jones and Bessie Zaban Jones, The Many Voices of Boston. *Boston: Little, Brown, 1975. Essay originally published in 1809.*

THINK ABOUT THIS

1. What do you think was Ames's opinion of human nature? Of himself?

2. Do you agree with Ames about the danger of demagogues?

The Supreme Court and States' Rights: John Marshall Hands Down an Opinion

During the early years of the United States, lawmakers and judges often faced the difficult question of where states' rights ended and the rights and powers of the federal government began. From the beginning of talk about a national government, a key issue had been conflict over whether the states should remain largely independent or should be largely controlled by a central authority. The Constitutional Convention did not completely solve the problem, and in the decades that followed, the states frequently tested their powers. One of the most important such tests occurred when the state of Maryland tried to tax a Baltimore bank, which happened to be a branch of the Bank of the United States, a federal bank. The bank refused to pay the tax. Maryland sued the bank. In 1819 the case went to the U.S. Supreme Court. Chief Justice John Marshall, one of the most influential of America's early judges and legal scholars, ruled that the bank did not have to pay the tax because Maryland had no authority over a federal institution, which belonged to all the people and not to any one state. This landmark decision in support of federal government dealt a blow to states' rights. A portion of Justice Marshall's opinion follows.

THE CONVENTION WHICH FRAMED the Constitution was indeed elected by the State legislatures. But the instrument, when it came from their hands, was a mere proposal, without obligation, or pretensions to it. It was reported to the then existing Congress of the United States, with a request that it might "be submitted to a Convention of Delegates, chosen in each State by the People thereof, under the recommendation of its Legislature, for their assent and ratification." This mode of proceeding was adopted; and by the Convention, by Congress, and by the State Legislatures, the instrument was submitted to the people. They acted

Wearing the long robe of his office, Chief Justice John Marshall of the U.S. Supreme Court swears in newly elected Andrew Jackson as president in March 1829. As chief justice from 1801 until his death in 1835, Marshall played a pivotal role in shaping the American judicial system.

upon it in the only manner in which they can act safely, effectively, and wisely, on such a subject, by assembling in Convention. It is true, they assembled in their several States—and where else should they have assembled? No political dreamer was ever wild enough to think of breaking down the lines which separate the States, and of compounding the American people into one common mass. Of consequence, when they act, they act in their States. But the measures they adopt do not, on that account, cease to be the measures of the people themselves, or become the measures of the State governments.

From these Conventions the Constitution derives its whole authority. The government proceeds directly from the people; is "ordained and established" in the name of the people; and is declared to be ordained, "in order to form a more perfect union, establish justice, ensure domestic tranquillity, and secure the blessings of liberty to themselves and to their posterity." The assent of the States, in their sovereign capacity, is implied in calling a Convention, and thus submitting that instrument to the people. But the people were at perfect liberty to accept or reject it; and their act was final. It required not the affirmance, and could not be negatived, by the State governments. The Constitution, when thus adopted, was of complete obligation, and bound the State sovereignties.

"The government proceeds directly from the people."

. . . After the most deliberate consideration, it is the unanimous and decided opinion of this Court, that the act to incorporate the Bank of the United States is a law made in pursuance of the Constitution, and is a part of the supreme law of the land.

The branches, proceeding from the same stock, and being conducive to the complete accomplishment of the object, are equally constitutional. It would have been unwise to locate them in the charter, and it would be unnecessarily inconvenient to employ the legislative power in making those subordinate arrangements. The great duties of the bank are prescribed, those duties require branches; and the bank itself may, we think, be safely trusted with the selection of places where those branches shall be fixed; reserving always to the government the right to require that a branch shall be located where it may be deemed necessary.

—*From Opinion of Chief Justice John Marshall in the Case of* McCulloch v. the State of Maryland *(1819), quoted in Charles W. Eliot, editor,* American Historical Documents, *Vol. 43. New York: Collier & Son, 1938.*

1. According to Marshall, why was the Constitution ratified, or approved, by the state legislatures, when it was supposed to reflect the will of "the people"?

2. This Supreme Court decision became the basis for many later decisions that favored the federal government over state governments. Can you explain why?

Chapter 5

African Americans and Slavery

AMERICANS HAD FOUGHT THE REVOLUTION in the name of liberty, yet some Americans were not free. From the earliest days of settlement, African slaves had provided much of the labor that made the colonies profitable. But there had always been some Americans who argued that slavery was wrong, and that view gained strength during and after the Revolution.

Antislavery feeling was strongest in the Northeast and in Pennsylvania; support for slavery was strongest in the South. The economy of the Southern states was based on plantation agriculture, the large-scale farming of export crops such as tobacco and cotton. Plantation farming demanded a great deal of labor, which slaves supplied. The Northeast, in contrast, relied on trade as well as agriculture, and its farms were not as large as those in the South. Slave labor was not essential to its prosperity, although some Northeasterners owned slaves. Pennsylvania's antislavery movement had religious roots. The colony had been founded by members of the religious sect known as the Society of Friends, or Quakers, whose faith led them to oppose enslavement.

The rift between the Southern slave states and the Northern free states that eventually culminated in the Civil War began earlier, during the New Republic period. Abolitionists, who opposed slavery, used many methods to help enslaved African Americans, as in this scene of a black man preparing to be mailed from the slave state of Virginia to the free state of Pennsylvania.

The end of American slavery began in Pennsylvania. Quakers founded the first antislavery society in 1775, and in 1780 the state government ordered the gradual freeing of slaves. Massachusetts declared slavery illegal in 1783. By 1804 New Hampshire, Connecticut, Rhode Island, New York, and New Jersey had passed antislavery laws. But although some Southern states limited the importing of new slaves, none had outlawed slavery itself. African Americans and their children born into slavery continued to be treated as property. This caused a problem at the Constitutional Convention. The Southern states wanted the slaves included in their populations so that they would have more delegates in Congress (seats in the House of Representatives are based on population size). Northerners, however, argued that the South could not both treat slaves as property *and* count them as citizens. In the end, the convention decided that each slave equaled three-fifths of a person in population counts. The South also demanded to be allowed to continue the slave trade, which many Northerners wanted to abolish entirely. The convention agreed that the slave trade could operate without federal interference for twenty years.

Many Americans feared that slavery would bring trouble for the United States in the future. One was Thomas Jefferson, who owned slaves. He foresaw that slavery would lead to conflict, either between slaves and their owners or between those who supported slavery and those who wanted to end it. Sadly, Jefferson was unable to prevent the coming problem. Half a century later, slavery would be one of the root causes of the bloodiest conflict in American history: the Civil War.

A Southerner Condemns Slavery

Southerners at the Constitutional Convention defended slavery and refused to give the federal government the power to regulate the slave trade. They were astonished when one of their own representatives, a respected Virginia statesman named George Mason, delivered a ringing speech that condemned slavery on moral and economic grounds.

THE PRESENT QUESTION CONCERNS NOT the importing states alone, but the whole Union. The evil of having slaves was experienced during the [Revolution]. Had the slaves been treated as they might have been by the [British], they would have proved dangerous instruments in their hands. But instead they were as foolish in dealing with the slaves as they were with the Tories. Maryland, Virginia, and North Carolina have prohibited the importation of slaves. But all this would be in vain if South Carolina and Georgia remained at liberty to import them. The West is calling out for slaves, and will fill their country if the states in the Lower South remain at liberty to import. Slavery discourages arts and manufactures. The poor despise labor when performed by slaves. Slavery prevents whites from immigrating, and produces the most pernicious effect on manners.

George Mason shocked his fellow Virginians when he delivered a speech that pointed out the moral evils and the economic flaws of slavery.

Tories
American colonists loyal to Great Britain during the Revolution

Every master of slaves is born a petty tyrant. They bring the judgment of Heaven on a country. As nations cannot be rewarded or punished in the next world they must be in this. By an inevitable chain of causes and effects providence punished national sins by national calamities. I hold it essential to every point of view that the General Government should have power to prevent the increase of slavery.

> "Every master of slaves is born a petty tyrant."

—From George Mason, quoted in Richard B. Morris, Witnesses at the Creation. New York: Holt, Rinehart and Winston, 1985.

THINK ABOUT THIS

What is Mason's economic argument against slavery? What is his moral argument?

David Walker Cries Out against Injustice

David Walker was a free black man living in Boston in the 1820s. He became one of the city's leading antislavery activists, and in 1829 he published a pamphlet called *David Walker's Appeal*. It brimmed with passionate criticism of both slavery and racism, the belief that one race is naturally inferior to another. Most disturbing of all to many white readers, Walker warned that if slavery continued in the South, black slaves would rise up violently against the whites. Many white people in both North and South saw the *Appeal* as a call to a slave rebellion, and the pamphlet was banned in the South. A passage from the pamphlet follows.

NEVER MAKE AN ATTEMPT to gain our freedom or *natural right,* from under our cruel oppressors and murderers, until you see your way clear—when that hour arrives and you move, be not afraid or dismayed; for be you assured that Jesus Christ the King of heaven and of earth who is the God of justice and of armies, will surely go before you. And those enemies who have for hundreds of years stolen our *rights,* and kept us ignorant of Him and His divine worship, he will remove. Millions of whom, are this day, so ignorant and avaricious, that they cannot conceive how God can have an attribute of justice, and show mercy to us because it pleased Him to make us black—which colour, Mr. Jefferson calls unfortunate! ! ! ! ! ! As though we are not as thankful to our God, for having made us as it pleased himself, as they, (the whites,) are for having made them white. They think because they hold us in their infernal chains of slavery, that we wish to be white, or their color—but they are dreadfully deceived—we wish to be just as it pleased our Creator to have made us, and no avaricious and

The opening of *David Walker's Appeal* shows a slave on a mountaintop, hands raised toward liberty and justice. Many white Americans, however, saw the *Appeal* as a direct threat to their safety.

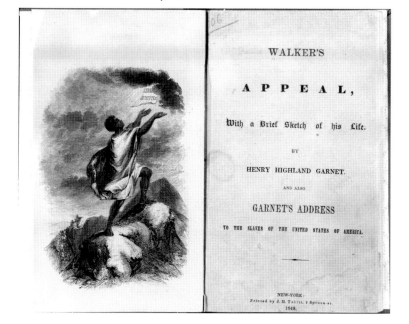

unmerciful wretches, have any business to make slaves of, or hold us in slavery. How would they like for us to make slaves of, and hold them in cruel slavery, and murder them as they do us?

—*From David Walker,* David Walker's Appeal, in Four Articles; Together with a Preamble, to the Coloured Citizens of the World, but in Particular, and Very Expressly, to Those of the United States of America, *third edition. Boston: Published by David Walker, 1830.*

THINK ABOUT THIS

1. Does this passage seem to be encouraging or approving violence?
2. Does Walker offer any justification for the use of violence?

William Lloyd Garrison Crusades against Slavery

Between the 1820s and the 1860s, black and white Americans who wanted to end slavery became an increasingly powerful force called the abolition movement. One of the country's leading abolitionists was William Lloyd Garrison, publisher of an antislavery newspaper called *The Liberator.* Even before founding his paper, Garrison had spoken out against slavery. In 1830, at the age of twenty-five, he wrote an essay attacking the usual excuses given by slaveholders for keeping their slaves.

IT IS MORALLY IMPOSSIBLE, I am convinced, for a slaveholder to reason correctly on the subject of slavery. His mind is warped by a thousand prejudices, and a thick cloud rests upon his mental vision. He was really taught to believe, that a certain class of beings were born for servitude, whom it is lawful to enthrall, and over whom he is authorized—not merely by the law of his native state, but by Jehovah himself—to hold unlimited dominion. . . . He discourses eloquently, it may be, upon the evils of this system—deprecates its continu-ance as a curse upon the country—shud-ders when he contemplates individual instances of barbarity—and rejoices in gradual emancipation. Interrogate him relative to his own practices, and you touch the apple of his eye. If not disposed to resent your freedom, he takes shelter in the ignorance and helplessness of his slaves; and, dextrously relinquishing the authority of an oppressor, assumes the amiableness of a philanthropist! "The poor creatures are penniless—benighted—without a home! Freedom would be a curse, rather than a blessing to them—they are happy now—why should I throw them upon an unpitying world?" Will a christian reason in this manner?

"It is morally impossible . . . for a slaveholder to reason correctly on the subject of slavery."

William Lloyd Garrison's paper *The Liberator*, founded in 1831, became a lasting force for abolition. (Garrison also attacked war, capital punishment, and alcohol in its pages.) In the first issue, Garrison declared, "I will not retreat a single inch—*and I will be heard.*"

Yes—if a christian can be a slaveholder—but the two characters differ so widely that I know not how they can unite in one man.

—From William Lloyd Garrison, quoted in Mason Lowance, editor, *Against Slavery: An Abolitionist Reader. New York: Penguin Books, 2000.*

THINK ABOUT THIS

How would you respond to a slaveholder who spoke in the manner quoted by Garrison?

Born into Slavery: The Narrative of Moses Roper

The attention won by *David Walker's Appeal* inspired other African Americans to tell their own stories and make their opinions known to the world. Many wrote or dictated their personal histories, which abolitionists collected and published as evidence of the cruelties of slavery. One such story was that of Moses Roper, a slave who escaped from the American South to England, where slavery was illegal. Roper, the child of a white slaveowner and the slaveowner's wife's black servant, was probably born in about 1800.

I WAS BORN IN NORTH CAROLINA, in Caswell County, I am not able to tell in what month or year. What I shall now relate, is what was told me by my mother and grandmother. A few months before I was born, my father married my mother's young mistress. As soon as my father's wife heard of my birth, she sent one of my mother's sisters to see whether I was white or black, and when my aunt had seen me she returned back as soon as she could, and told her mistress that I was white, and resembled Mr. Roper very much. Mr. Roper's wife not being pleased with this report, she got a large club-stick and knife, and hastened to the place in which my mother was confined. She went into my mother's room with a full intention to murder me with her knife and club, but as she was going to stick the knife into me, my grandmother happening to come in, caught the knife and saved my life. But as well as I can recollect from what my mother told me, my father sold her and myself, soon after the confinement. . . . The way they divide their slaves is this: they write the names of different slaves on a small piece of paper, and put it into a box, and let them all draw. I think that Mr. Durham drew my mother, and Mr. Fowler drew me, we were separated a considerable distance, I cannot say how far.

"She went into my mother's room with a full intention to murder me."

—*From Moses Roper,* The Narrative of Moses Roper, *quoted in Alan Govenar, editor,* African American Frontiers: Slave Narratives and Oral Histories. *Santa Barbara: ABC-CLIO, 2000. Originally published in 1837.*

THINK ABOUT THIS

What cruel or abusive elements of slavery does Roper's story highlight?

A Midnight Escape: John Malvin Leads Slaves to Freedom

African American John Malvin was born free in Virginia. In 1827 he moved to the Ohio River valley to escape the racism of the South. He discovered that although blacks in Ohio did suffer from racism, they were forming their own communities there. In time

Malvin became a respected citizen of Cincinnati. Late in his life he published his autobiography, in which he told of how he had helped slaves escape years before.

DURING MY RESIDENCE IN CINCINNATI, I was frequently in the habit of visiting the boats and steamers on the Ohio River, as I was fond of looking at them, especially the machinery. On one of these occasions I visited two boats, and then a third boat which was called the "Criterion." The boats lay close to each other, and on board of the "Criterion" there were thirty slaves bound for the southern market. I was standing on the permanent deck of the "Criterion" when a woman of interesting appearance passed near me, coming from the hurricane deck. I spoke to her and found her name to be Susan Hall, and that she was from the same county where I was born. I had never seen her before, but my mother had often seen her, and spoken of her to me. She told me that she had two children aboard, a boy and a girl. I asked her if she would like to be free. She said she would like it very much. I had to leave off talking with her then, as the watch was very strict, and told her I had to go over into Kentucky, but would return that same night. So great was my abhorrence of slavery, that I was willing to run any risk to accomplish the liberation of a slave. I crossed over into Kentucky, and returned between sundown and dark, and went aboard of the boat. There I remained until about one o'clock, when the woman made her appearance with one of her children. She told me that things were so situated that she could not get her girl without discovery, and we were obliged to leave without the girl. . . . The gang-plank at the stern was drawn in, and there was no means of exit from the boat except by the forward gang plank. It was impossible, however, for us to escape at that place, as two men were posted there with guns as watch. On looking around, however, I found there was a small boat belonging to the "Criterion" in the water at the stern. I concluded to make use of this

Cincinnati in 1835, as seen across the Ohio River from Kentucky by landscape painter John Caspar Wild. From a steamboat like those shown here, John Malvin helped several slaves escape into Ohio, a free state.

boat for the purpose of effecting the escape. I assisted the woman and her boy into the little boat and untied it from the "Criterion." There was another large steamer astern of the "Criterion," and I shot the little boat quickly out under the bow of this other steamer, and made it appear as though I was leaving the steamer and not the "Criterion." The guards were deluded by this ruse, and paid no attention to us, thinking we came from the other boat. The risk, however, was very great. We could see the barrels of their guns glisten in the moonlight. I effected a landing and brought them to a place of safety. Then I returned and succeeded in getting aboard of the "Criterion" again, and in the same manner I succeeding in effecting the escape of two young men and a young woman.

—From John Malvin, Autobiography of John Malvin, *quoted in*
Allan Peskin, editor, North into Freedom. *Cleveland, OH: Press of Western
Reserve University, 1966. Originally published in 1879.*

THINK ABOUT THIS

How would you describe Malvin's actions? Why did he do what he did?

A tomahawk-wielding Indian charges at frontiersman Natty Bumppo, the hero of five action-filled novels by James Fenimore Cooper that make up the popular *Leather-Stockings Tales*. Writing in the first half of the nineteenth century, Cooper captured the imagination of American audiences eager for heroic tales of the young nation's past. Cooper both glorified the building of America and criticized some aspects of society. His frontiersman and many of his Indian characters are brave, noble figures who love the grandeur of the wilderness, while settlers in the books represent not just civilization and order but also, sometimes, greed and pettiness. This scene from *The Deerslayer* was painted by N. C. Wyeth (1882–1945), who illustrated many classics of fiction.

Chapter 6

Arts and Sciences

INDEPENDENCE FOR THE UNITED STATES meant more than political freedom from Great Britain—it also meant cultural freedom. During the colonial era, American arts and sciences had been measured against British standards. After the Revolution, however, citizens of the new republic felt a growing pride in the fact that their accomplishments were *American* achievements.

One important area of scientific activity was natural history, or the earth sciences. Biology (the study of living things), geology (the study of rocks), and meteorology (the study of climate and weather) were all part of the territory of the natural historian, or naturalist. British and European naturalists had a long tradition of visiting North America to marvel at the region's landscapes and creatures. Yet while these wonders were located within a British colony, they were seen as being somehow British. Once the United States became an independent nation, Americans delighted in the thought that their country's land and wildlife were as extraordinary and unique as its democratic government. Naturalists from other countries continued to make scientific pilgrimages to North America, but American naturalists began to make major contributions to the study of their own country.

Americans also produced new developments in the practical sciences, such as mechanics. Among the country's founders were two men who invented a number of useful devices: Benjamin Franklin and Thomas Jefferson. Other Americans also created new tools and machines, many of which were designed to make agriculture and industry more productive. For example, Eli Whitney's cotton gin completely changed the process of cleaning cotton. The machine did not simply make the task easier than cleaning cotton by hand—it allowed one person to do the work of fifty. To many Americans of the time, such inventions became symbols of American genius and progress.

Americans also took pride in their artists and writers. In the decades after the Revolution, people made a point of favoring the works of Americans over those produced by the British and French, who had long set the standards for art and literature. Many of the most popular literary works of the time dealt with colonial life, the Revolution, or other subjects from American history. Citizens of the young nation had a great appetite for tales about their country's past and its birth.

Exploring for Science: William Bartram in Georgia

One of the first American-born scientists was William Bartram, a naturalist who was especially interested in botany, the study of plants. The son of botanist John Bartram, who was born in England but settled in Pennsylvania when it was still a British colony, William Bartram made several journeys through the Carolinas, Georgia, and Florida, studying, drawing, and collecting plants. His 1792 book about his travels contained much scientific information, but it also celebrated the region's wild beauty and natural wonders. In this passage he tells of a journey on Georgia's Altamaha River, using the elaborate, poetic language that was a style of his times.

WHEN WEARIED WITH WORKING MY CANOE against the impetuous current (which becomes stronger by reason of the mighty floods of the river, with collected force, pressing through the first hilly ascents, where the shores on each side present to view rocky cliffs rising above the surface of the water, in nearly flat horizontal masses, washed smooth by the descending floods, and which appear to be a composition, or concrete, of sandy lime-stone) I resigned my bark to the friendly current, reserving to myself the controul of the helm. My progress was rendered delightful by the sylvan elegance of the groves, cheerful meadows, and high distant forests, which in grand order presented themselves to view. The winding banks of the river, and the high projecting promontories, unfolded fresh scenes of grandeur and sublimity. The deep forests and distant hills re-echoed the cheering social lowings of domestic herds. The air was filled with the loud and shrill whooping of the wary sharp-sighted crane. Behold, on yon decayed, defoliated cypress tree, a solitary wood-pelican, dejectedly

> *"My progress was rendered delightful by the sylvan elegance of the groves, cheerful meadows, and high distant forests."*

William Bartram, one of the leading scientists of the young republic, specialized in the study of plants but also took an interest in birds and other creatures.

perched upon its utmost elevated spire; he there, like an ancient venerable sage, sets himself up as a mark of derision, for the safety of his kindred tribes. The crying-bird, another faithful guardian, screaming in the gloomy thickets, warns the feathered tribes of approaching peril. And the plumage of the swift sailing squadrons of Spanish curlews (white as the immaculate robe of innocence) gleams in the cerulean skies.

Thus secure and tranquil, and meditating on the marvellous scenes of primitive nature, as yet unmodified by the hand of man, I gently descended the peaceful stream, on whose polished surface were depicted the mutable shadows from its pensile banks; while myriads of finny inhabitants sported in its pellucid floods.

The glorious sovereign of day, clothed in light refulgent, rolling on his gilded chariot, hastened to revisit the western realms. Grey pensive eve now admonished us of gloomy night's hasty approach: I was roused by care to seek a place of secure repose, ere darkness came on.

—*From William Bartram,* Travels through North and South Carolina, Georgia, East and West Florida, *1792. Facsimile edition, Charlottesville, VA: University Press of Virginia, 1980.*

1. What symbolic meaning or emotional importance does Bartram give to natural objects and events?

2. Why do you think he interprets the natural world in this way instead of simply describing its features?

"Every thing that is curious of this Country": America's First Museum

In 1786, artist Charles Willson Peale of Philadelphia opened America's first museum in his house. His collection, small at first, included portraits that he had painted and specimens of plants, animals, fossils, rocks, and what Peale called "natural curiosities." The first passage below is from a letter Peale wrote to George Washington that year, describing his goals. The second is from a newspaper announcement of 1792 in which Peale invited American citizens to contribute specimens and money to his museum. For Peale, the museum was more than a collection of artistic and scientific objects—it was an expression of national pride.

I HAVE LATELY UNDERTAKEN to form a Museum and have acquired the means of preserving in the natural forms, Birds, Beasts, and Fish, my Intention is to collect every thing that is curious of this Country, and to arrange them in the best manner I am able, to make the Collection amusing and In[s]tructive, thereby hoping to retain with us many things realy curious which would otherwise be sent to Europe.

America has . . . a conspicuous advantage over all other countries, *from the novelty of its vast territories*. But a small number is yet

Charles Willson Peale of Philadelphia painted this picture of himself in the museum he created. Peale hoped to promote excellence in both the arts and sciences in the United States, freeing Americans from dependence upon European expertise.

known of the amazing variety of animal, vegetable, and mineral productions, in our forests of 1000 miles, our inland seas, our many rivers, that roll through several states, and mingle with the ocean.

A Museum stored with these treasures must indeed become one of the first in the world; the more so, as the principal naturalists in Europe, will be anxious to acquire our productions, by an exchange of whatever is most valuable in their respective countries and foreign colonies.

—*Quoted in Christopher Irmscher,* The Poetics of Natural History: From John Bartram to William James. *New Brunswick, NJ: Rutgers University Press, 1999.*

THINK ABOUT THIS

1. Peale tells Washington why it is especially important to create an American museum. What is the reason?

2. What factors did Peale think could make an American museum one of the finest in the world?

Inventing Modern Industry:
Eli Whitney's Cotton Gin

Born in Massachusetts in 1765, Eli Whitney was one of the inventors who changed the way Americans worked. In 1793 he produced his best-known invention, a machine for ginning cotton, or separating the usable fiber from the seeds and stems. Whitney later became a firearms manufacturer, and the methods he introduced in his factory included using interchangeable parts and dividing a task into a series of small steps, each performed by one person who did the same job over and over. Other American inventors, including Henry Ford, later adopted these principles of mass production. As for Whitney's cotton gin, other inventors illegally copied its design, and Whitney never profited as much from it as he had hoped he would. A letter to his father in 1794 reveals those high hopes.

IT IS WITH NO SMALL SATISFACTION that I have it in my power to inform you that I am in good health. I have just returned from Philadelphia. My business there was to lodge a Model of my [cotton gin] and receive a Patent for it. I accomplished everything agreeable to my wishes. I had the satisfaction to hear it declared by a number of the first men in America that my machine is the most perfect &

" . . . the most perfect & the most valuable invention that has ever appeared in this Country."

the most valuable invention that has ever appeared in this Country. . . . Though I have as yet expended much more money than the profits of the machine have been heretofore, and am at present a little pressed for money, I am by no means in the least discouraged. And I shall probably gain some honour as well as profit by the Invention. It was said by one of the most respectable Gentlemen in N. Haven [Connecticut] that he would rather be the author of the invention than to be prime minister of England. But I mean not to be eleated by my success so much as to be vain.

—From Eli Whitney, letter of 1794 to his father, quoted in Jeannette Mirsky and Allan Nevins, The World of Eli Whitney. New York: Macmillan, 1952.

THINK ABOUT THIS

What did Whitney hope to gain by inventing the cotton gin?

An Early American Play: Songs from *The Indian Princess*

James Nelson Barker was born in Philadelphia in 1784, the year after the American Revolution ended. Before entering politics he tried his hand at writing plays. *The Indian Princess,* about the legend of a Native American girl named Pocahontas and a settler named Captain John Smith, was staged in Philadelphia in 1808. Twelve years later a British theater group produced the play in London under the title *Pocahontas,* and historians now think it was the first American play staged in England. *The Indian Princess* set a fashion for plays featuring Native American characters, although Barker does not seem to have known much about Indian speech or customs. In the first of these two songs from the play, Pocahontas croons a mournful, flowery love poem. In the second, a character named Walter sings the praises of Captain Smith, a hero in matters of Venus and Mars (love

American artists often used subjects from colonial history, such as Pocahontas, a real Indian whose story is entangled with legends. This image of her is almost a primary source— it is based on a portrait painted from life in 1616, the year before her death.

and war). Remarkably, Barker managed to create a rhyme for "Pocahontas."

Pocahontas:
When the midnight of absence the day-dream pervading
    Distills the chill dew o'er the bosom of love,
Oh, how fast then the gay tints of nature are fading,
    How harsh seems the music of joy in the grove.
While the tender flow'r droops till return of the light
Steeped in tear drops that fall from the eye of the night.

Walter:
Captain Smith is a man of might,
In Venus's soft wars or in Mars's bloody fight,
For of widow, or wife, or of damsel bright
    A bold blade, you know, is all the dandy.
. . .
Captain Smith, from the foaming seas,
From pirates, and shipwreck, and miseries,
In a French lady's arms found a haven of ease;
    Her name—pshaw, from memory quite gone 't has.
    And on this savage shore,
    Where his falchion stained with gore,
      His noble heart

falchion
type of sword

The savage dart
Had quivered through,
But swifter flew
To his heart the pretty princess, Pocahontas.

—*From James Nelson Barker,* The Indian Princess,
quoted in Grenville Vernon, Yankee Doodle-Doo: A Collection of Songs
of the Early American Stage. *New York: Payson and Clarke, 1927.*

THINK ABOUT THIS

1. How would you describe the tone and content of Pocahontas's song?
2. What does Walter seem to admire most about Captain Smith?

Creating an American Hero: Natty Bumppo in *The Pioneers*

James Fenimore Cooper (1789–1851) was one the most popular American authors of the early republic. His most successful works were romantic adventures that glorified the French and Indian War, the Revolutionary War, and other heroic episodes in America's past. Cooper's novel *The Pioneers,* published in 1823, introduced the character of Natty Bumppo, also called Leatherstocking, the Pathfinder, and Hawkeye. Later novels would describe Bumppo's early career, but Cooper set *The Pioneers* in 1793, when the once-great Leatherstocking was an old man watching the wilderness being swallowed up by towns, rules, and the other business of civilization. Hauled to court and fined for killing a deer out of season, Bumppo addresses a moving plea to the judge.

"HEAR ME, MARMADUKE TEMPLE," interrupted the old man, with melancholy earnestness, "and hear reason. I've travelled these mountains when you was no judge, but an infant in your mother's arms; and I feel as if I had a right and a privilege to travel them ag'in afore I die. Have you forgot the time that you come on to the lake shore, when there wasn't even a [jail] to lodge in; and didn't I give you my own bearskin to sleep on, and the fat of a noble buck to satisfy the cravings of your hunger? Yes, yes—you thought it no sin then to kill a deer! And this I did, though I had no reason to love you, for you had never done anything but harm to them that loved and sheltered me. And now, will you shut me up in your dungeons to pay me for my kindness? A hundred dollars! where should I get the money? No, no— there's them that says hard things of you, Marmaduke Temple, but you an't so bad as to wish to see an old man die in a prison because he stood up for the right. Come, friend, let me pass: it's long sin' I've been used to such crowds, and I crave to be in the woods ag'in. Don't fear me, Judge—I bid you not to fear me, for if there's beaver enough left on the streams, or the buckskins will sell for a shilling apiece, you shall have the last penny of the fine. Where are ye, pups! come away, dogs! come away! we have a grievous toil to do for years, but it shall be done—yes, yes, I've promised it, and it shall be done!"

—From James Fenimore Cooper, The Pioneers, *in Allan Nevins, editor,*
The Leatherstocking Saga. *New York: Pantheon Books, 1954.*

THINK ABOUT THIS

Bumppo makes both an emotional and a practical argument for his release. What is the emotional argument? What is the practical argument?

Americans celebrate "Yankee know-how" as DeWitt Clinton, governor of New York, pours water from Lake Erie into the Atlantic Ocean at the opening of the Erie Canal in 1825. The canal was an engineering achievement that linked the two bodies of water and connected the interior of the United States with major shipping ports on the East Coast.

Chapter 7

The Age of
New Possibilities

THE EFFECTS OF THE REVOLUTIONARY WAR shaped the way Americans felt and thought and acted for many years after the fighting ended. The colonies had stood up to Europe's leading power. Their ragged, penniless army and their pitifully small navy had humbled Britain's much larger and better-equipped fighting forces. It was an amazing and inspiring victory, as though a dog had outwitted and outfought an elephant. As if that weren't enough, Americans had then created a new kind of government "of the people, by the people, and for the people," a government that many Americans believed was the best that had ever existed. After these achievements, the citizens of the new nation felt that there was nothing they couldn't do.

The young republic brimmed with confidence and the excitement of making a new beginning, of turning a page in the book of history. Although many traditional customs and rules remained strongly in force, people also began to enjoy doing things in their own American way rather than slavishly following British or European models. The conditions of everyday life in the United States were often much more rugged, even harsh, than those in England or France, partly because America had not yet developed many factories to manufacture such things as glass, paper, and fine cloth and partly because some Americans lived on the frontier, far from schools and markets. Americans living in rustic circumstances, however, took a stubborn pride in their ability to "do without" or "make do." Their sense of toughness and self-reliance became one strand of what Americans liked to think of as their national character.

Another strand was the combination of energy and skill that was often referred to as "enterprise." Many Americans liked to imagine that their nation was a bustling beehive of productive activity compared with the old, tired nations of Europe. People began using terms such as "Yankee know-how" to describe Americans' ability to solve problems and get things done. The early United States had many men and women who saw the world in terms of opportunities and possibilities—everything from creating new businesses to reshaping the very landscape of America itself.

"Those Active, Interesting Girls": The Women of the Lowell Factories

A new era in American industry began in 1814, when a New Englander named Francis Cabot Lowell opened the first of many textile mills, or cloth-making factories, in Massachusetts. These mills had two revolutionary features. First, they introduced the modern factory system, with all stages of cloth-making carried out under one roof in an organized process. Second, they employed mostly young, unmarried women, who were housed at

Carrying lunch pails and baskets, employees—many of them young women—throng outside a New England factory. Although some call such factory work anonymous mass labor in an impersonal setting, many of the "Lowell girls" and other female employees of the time saw it as a new opportunity to be productive and independent.

the mills. Some modern historians view these "Lowell girls" as exploited laborers who were paid lower wages than men for hard work in uncomfortable conditions. But others, including some of the Lowell girls themselves, saw factory work as a new and exciting chance for women to earn money and achieve independence. In *A New England Girlhood,* Lucy Larcom recalled her time as a Lowell girl.

THE GIRLS WHO TOILED TOGETHER at Lowell were clearing away a few weeds from the overgrown track of independent labor for other women. They practically said, by numbering themselves among factory girls, that in our country no real odium could be attached to any honest toil that any self-respecting woman might undertake.

I regard it as one of the privileges of my youth that I was permitted to grow up among those active, interesting girls, whose lives were not mere echoes of other lives, but had principle and purpose distinctly their own. Their vigor of character was a natural phenomenon. The New Hampshire girls who came to Lowell were descendants of the sturdy backwoodsmen who settled that State scarcely a hundred years before. Their grandmothers had suffered the hardships of frontier life, had known the horrors of savage warfare when the beautiful valleys of the Connecticut and the Merrimack were threaded with Indian trails from Canada to the white settlements. Those young women did justice to their inheritance. They were earnest and capable; ready to undertake anything that was worth doing. My dreamy, indolent nature was shamed into activity among them. They gave me a larger, firmer ideal of womanhood.

> *"Their vigor of character was a natural phenomenon."*

—*From Lucy Larcom,* A New England Girlhood.
Boston and New York: Houghton Mifflin, 1889.

THINK ABOUT THIS

1. According to Larcom, how did the Lowell girls help all women?
2. What did she mean by the statement that the Lowell girls' lives were "not mere echoes of other lives"? Whose "other lives"?
3. What effect did working in the mills have on Larcom, and why?

An Englishwoman Describes Americans: Frances Trollope

Frances Trollope, an Englishwoman who lived in the United States from 1827 to 1831, held a view of American women very different from Lucy Larcom's. Trollope came to America partly to see the country and partly to mend her family's troubled finances. She opened a store in Cincinnati, Ohio, but also traveled in other parts of the land. Upon returning to England she wrote *Domestic Manners of the Americans,* which presented American life and citizens as rude, crude, and inferior to those of England. Americans were outraged and heaped scorn on Trollope, but her book sold very well on both sides of the Atlantic. Her son Anthony Trollope, who became a best-selling author, later said, "Her volumes were very bitter, but they were very clever, and they saved the family from ruin." Here is an excerpt from her book.

[I]F THE CONDITION OF THE LABOURER be not superior to that of the English peasant, that of his wife and daughters is incomparably worse. It is they who are indeed the slaves of the soil. One has but to look at the wife of an American cottager, and ask her age, to be convinced that the life she leads is one of hardship, privation, and labour. It is rare to see a woman in this station who has reached the age of thirty, without losing every trace of youth and beauty. You continually see

> "It is rare to see a woman ... who has reached the age of thirty, without losing every trace of youth and beauty."

Frances Trollope (*right*) had a very low opinion of American manners and thought most Americans were crude. Among the illustrations in her book on the subject was one of a drunkard.

women with infants on their knee, that you feel sure are their grandchildren, till some convincing proof of the contrary is displayed. Even the young girls, though often with lovely features, look pale, thin, and haggard. I do not remember to have seen in any single instance among the poor, a specimen of the plump, rosy, laughing physiognomy so common among our cottage girls. The horror of domestic service, which the reality of slavery, and the fable of equality, have generated, excludes the young women from that sure and most comfortable resource of decent English girls; and the consequence is, that with a most irreverent freedom of manner to the parents, the daughters are, to the full extent of the word, domestic slaves. This condition, which no periodical merry-making, no village *fete* [party], ever occurs to cheer, is only changed for the still sadder burdens of a teeming wife. They marry very young; in fact, in no rank of life do you meet with young women in that delightful period of existence between childhood and marriage, wherein, if only tolerably well spent, so much useful information is gained, and the character takes a sufficient degree of firmness to support with dignity the more important parts of wife and mother.

The slender, childish thing, without vigour of mind or body, is made to stem a sea of troubles that dims her young eye and makes her cheek grow pale, even before nature has given it the last beautiful finish of the full-grown woman. "We shall get along," is the answer in full, for all that can be said in way of advice to a boy and girl who take it into their heads to go before a magistrate and "get married." And they do get along, till sickness overtakes them, by means perhaps of borrowing a kettle from one and a tea-pot from another; but intemperance, idleness, or sickness will, in one week, plunge those who are even getting along well into utter destitution; and where this happens, they are completely without resource.

—*From Frances Trollope,* Domestic Manners of the Americans. *New York: Oxford University Press, 1984. Originally published in 1832.*

THINK ABOUT THIS

1. How did the concept of liberty affect the daughters of working-class Americans?
2. What is Trollope's opinion of American marriage customs?

An Unusual Business: The Ice Trade

Edwin Basil Hall was a sea captain from Scotland who traveled in the United States in the late 1820s. He later wrote a book about his experiences in America. While in Boston he became aware of an unusual local business venture: the ice trade. Hall described an entrepreneur—someone who had a bold new idea and, with patience and persistence, turned it into a profitable business. Entrepreneurship was to become a key part of Americans' sense of their national identity. The Boston ice trade, which filled a need in the era before refrigeration and air-conditioning, was an early example of successful entrepreneurship. Hall tells how it worked in the selection that follows.

IN THE COURSE OF THE DAY, a gentleman gave us a very interesting account of a species of commerce peculiar, at least on so great a scale, as far as I know, to the United States—I mean the transport by sea of large quantities of ice. This trade is carried on chiefly to the Havannah in the West Indies, and to Charleston in South Carolina. Upwards of twenty years ago, a gentleman of most praiseworthy enterprise hit upon this idea, which he has pursued ever since with great activity, and eventually with success, though in its progress he had many difficulties to encounter. There is no particular care taken to preserve the ice on board, except that the ship is cased inside with planks to prevent it coming in contact with the ceiling. The ice, cut into cubes 18 inches each way, is carefully packed by hand. The loss by melting on the voyage is sometimes one-third of the whole, though it often arrives with no perceptible diminution. My informant told me, that when the ice is embarked in winter, with the thermometer at Zero, or below it, and the ship has the good fortune to sail with a brisk, cold, northerly wind, not a single pound of the cargo is lost. As the temperature of the ice on shipping it is sometimes 30 degrees below the point at which it begins to melt, a considerable expenditure of cold must take place, and consequently a certain amount of time elapse, before it

> " . . . if the ship be then met by a southerly wind against her . . . the whole slippery cargo is apt to find its way overboard."

begins to lose weight; so that, if the voyage be short, the entire cargo is saved. On the other hand, if it be embarked from the ice-houses of Boston in July, with the thermometer at 80° or 90°, the melting process will have already commenced; and if the ship be then met by a southerly wind against her, or get drifted into that immense current of hot water flowing out of the great Bay of Mexico, known by the name of the Gulf Stream, the whole slippery cargo is apt to find its way overboard—via the pumps—before the voyage is half over.

Of late years, no less than three thousand tons of ice have been shipped annually from Boston to the South, a fact which affords a curious illustration of the power of commerce to equalise and bring together, as it were, the most distant climates. We are so familiar with the ordinary case of oranges, which we buy on the lowest stalls for three-a-penny, that we almost forget they are not natives to our own soil, and that it is far beyond the reach of art to make them so. But it must go hard with the fancy of a person who sees it for the first time, if he be not struck with the fact of his being able to buy ice almost as cheap in the streets of Charleston, as he can in those of Quebec.

—*From Captain Edwin Basil Hall,* Travels in North America in the Years 1827 and 1828, *Edinburgh, 1830. Quoted in Howard Mumford Jones and Bessie Zaban Jones, editors,* The Many Voices of Boston. *Boston: Little, Brown, 1975.*

THINK ABOUT THIS

1. What circumstances determined whether the voyage of an ice trader would succeed or fail?

2. Hall cited ice and oranges as examples of how business carried goods far from the places where they naturally occur. Can you think of examples from other periods in American history? From the present?

Catherine Beecher's Suggestions for Improving Education

Catherine Beecher's family was deeply interested in social problems. One of her sisters, Harriet Beecher Stowe, wrote *Uncle Tom's Cabin* to highlight the evils of slavery, but Catherine Beecher focused on education and the role of women. In 1829 she published *Suggestions Respecting Improvements in Education,* which pointed out that men were trained for respected professions such as law and medicine. Women, however,

Two young women study geography at a girls' school. They may have been training to become teachers, one of the few professions open to women at the time.

seldom received either respect or advanced educations, even though most teachers were women. Beecher did not call for women's rights as the term is used today. She believed that teaching was the only profession suitable for women, and she did not think that women should seek full equality with men. But, at a time when some women were just beginning to question their roles in a society dominated by men, Beecher argued that women deserved better educations and that mothers and teachers deserved respect for teaching young minds and forming young characters.

IT IS TO *MOTHERS,* AND TO *TEACHERS,* that the world is to look for the character which is to be enstamped on each succeeding generation, for it is to them that the great business of education is almost exclusively committed. And will it not appear by examination that neither mothers nor teachers have ever been properly educated for their profession[?] What is the *profession of a Woman*? Is it not to form immortal minds, and to watch, to nurse, and to rear the bodily system. . . ?

"What is the 'profession of a Woman?'"

. . . If it be claimed that it is necessary to the *improvement of the several arts and sciences,* that *man* should turn his attention exclusively to some one particular department, and thus prevent the equilibrium of character desired, it may be granted to *one* sex, but it is not necessary for *woman.* On the contrary, *a well balanced mind* is the greatest and best preparative for her varied and complicated duties. Woman, in her sphere of usefulness, has an almost equal need of all the several faculties. She needs the discrimination, the solidity, and the force of character which the cultivation of the reasoning powers confers; she needs the refinement of taste, the chastened glow of imagination, the powers of quick perception, and of ready invention. Which of these shall we say a woman may dispense with in preparing herself for future duties[?]

—From Catherine Beecher, Suggestions Respecting Improvements in Education, *1829. Reprinted in J. Boydston, M. Kelley, and A. Margolis,* The Limits of Sisterhood. *Chapel Hill, NC: University of North Carolina Press, 1988.*

THINK ABOUT THIS

1. What, according to Beecher, is a woman's most important duty? Do you agree?

2. Does Beecher see a drawback in educating someone for "one particular department" or professional specialty?

"Unrivalled Work": Philip Freneau's Poem about the Erie Canal

The State of New York sponsored a magnificent celebration when the 363-mile-long Erie Canal opened for business in 1825. For the first time, canal boats would carry passengers and goods between the Hudson River and the Great Lakes, making trade between America's East Coast and its interior much easier. Newspapers blossomed with articles praising American engineering skill and can-do spirit. Even before the canal was completed, Philip Freneau, who had founded the Republican newspaper *National Gazette* in

A print based on an 1829 watercolor drawing shows the Erie Canal cutting through the New York countryside. The canal, which transformed the landscape and created new possibilities for trade and travel, was the perfect symbol of its era, a time when Americans proudly believed that they could do anything.

Philadelphia in 1791, had celebrated the feat. His poem "Stanzas on the Great Western Canal of the State of New York" appeared in a New Jersey paper in 1822. It captures a feeling shared by many Americans in the 1820s: the belief that the United States was so mighty, it could even change the course of nature. Any vision could become reality in this land of new possibilities.

From *Erie's* shores to *Hudson's*
    stream
The unrivalled work would endless
    seem;
Would millions for the work demand,
And half depopulate the land.
    To Fancy's view, what years must run,
What ages, till the task is done!
Even trust, severe would seem to say,
One hundred years must pass away:—
    Three years elapsed, behold it done!
A work from Nature's *chaos* won;
By hearts of oak and hands of toil
The Spade inverts the rugged soil
A work, that may remain secure
While suns exist and Moons endure. . . .
    Ye patrons of this bold design
Who *Erie* to the *Atlantic* join,
To you be every honour paid—
No time shall see your fame decayed:—
Through gloomy groves you traced the plan,
The rude abodes of savage man.
    Ye Prompters of a work so vast
That may for years, for centuries last;
Where Nature toiled to bar the way
You mark'd her steps, but changed her way.
    Ye Artists, who, with skillful hand,
Conduct such rivers through the land,
Proceed!—and in your bold career

*"A work
from Nature's
chaos won."*

May every Plan as wise appear,
As *this,* which joins to *Hudson's* wave
What Nature to *St. Lawrence* gave.

—From Philip Freneau, *"Stanzas on the Great Western Canal of the State of New York,"* quoted in Lionel D. Wyld, Low Bridge! Folklore and the Erie Canal. *Syracuse, NY: Syracuse University Press, 1962.*

THINK ABOUT THIS

1. What does Freneau seem to admire most about the Erie Canal?

2. Does he make any exaggerated or unrealistic claims? If so, what are they?

Time Line

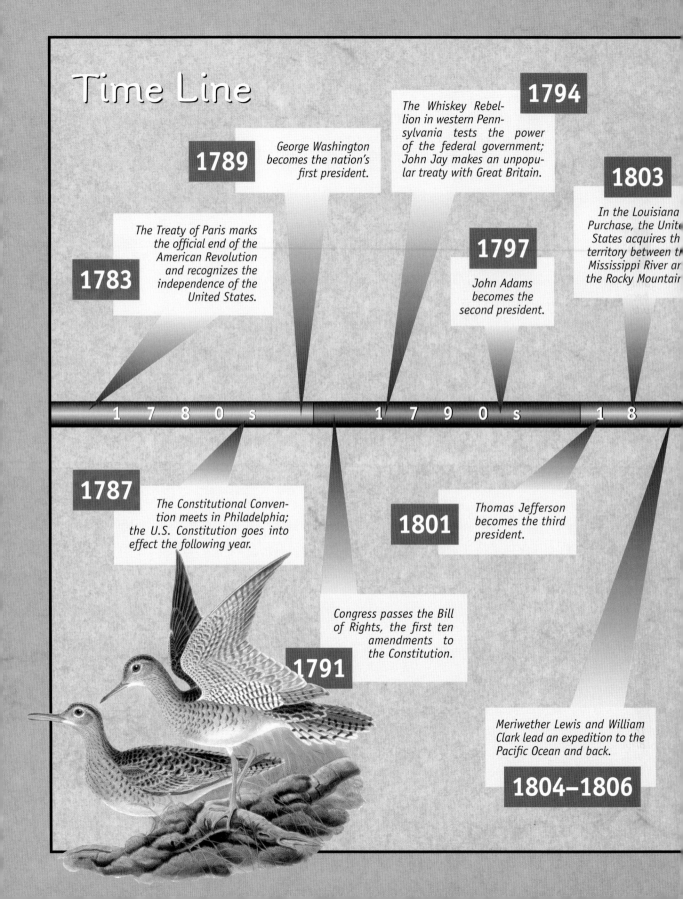

1789
George Washington becomes the nation's first president.

1794
The Whiskey Rebellion in western Pennsylvania tests the power of the federal government; John Jay makes an unpopular treaty with Great Britain.

1803
In the Louisiana Purchase, the Unite States acquires th territory between th Mississippi River ar the Rocky Mountair

1783
The Treaty of Paris marks the official end of the American Revolution and recognizes the independence of the United States.

1797
John Adams becomes the second president.

1 7 8 0 s   1 7 9 0 s   1 8

1787
The Constitutional Convention meets in Philadelphia; the U.S. Constitution goes into effect the following year.

1801
Thomas Jefferson becomes the third president.

Congress passes the Bill of Rights, the first ten amendments to the Constitution.
1791

Meriwether Lewis and William Clark lead an expedition to the Pacific Ocean and back.
1804–1806

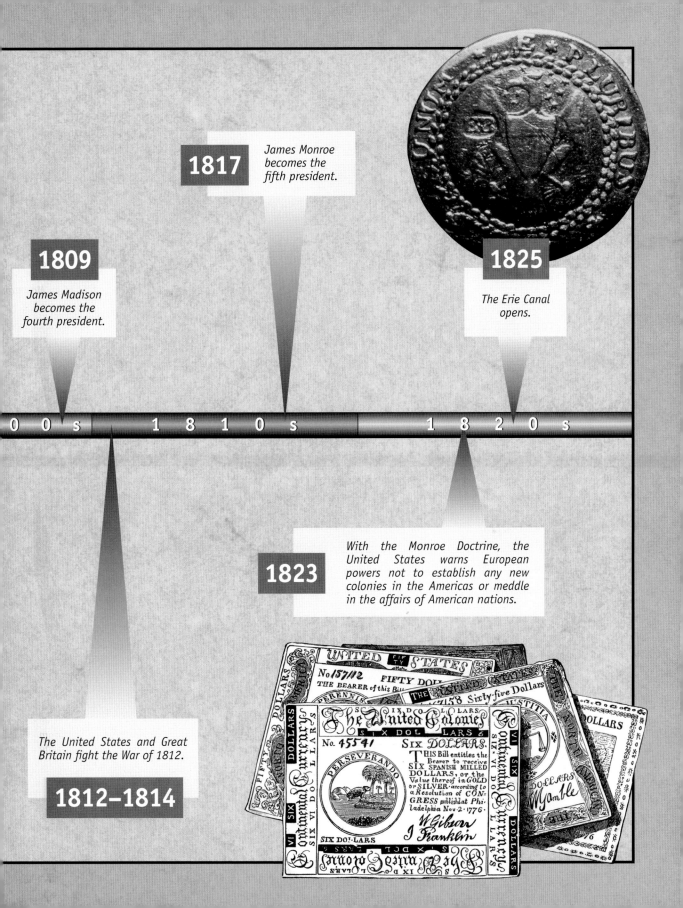

1817
James Monroe becomes the fifth president.

1809
James Madison becomes the fourth president.

1825
The Erie Canal opens.

0 0 s   1 8 1 0 s   1 8 2 0 s

1823
With the Monroe Doctrine, the United States warns European powers not to establish any new colonies in the Americas or meddle in the affairs of American nations.

The United States and Great Britain fight the War of 1812.

1812–1814

Glossary

avaricious greedy

benighted backward or ignorant; literally, covered in darkness

colony territory outside a nation's borders but claimed or settled by that nation

confederation loose association of independent states joined for some purpose, such as self-defense or trade

demagogue political leader who rouses public opinion by appealing to prejudices or making false promises

doctrine principle or statement of belief

pernicious harmful, destructive

physiognomy face or features

pillory structure used for public punishment or humiliation, made of a wooden frame with holes through which the head and hands are fastened

political party group of like-minded voters who support the same candidates

republic government in which citizens choose those who will govern them

sedition treason or attempt to undermine the state or government

wampum form of currency made of shells and used by Native Americans

To Find Out More

BOOKS

Dougan, Clark, Samuel Lipsman, and the editors of Boston Publishing Company. *A Nation Divided.* Boston: Boston Publishing Company, 1984.

Banfield, Susan. *James Madison.* New York: Franklin Watts, 1986.

Bosco, Peter. *The War of 1812.* Brookfield, CT: Millbrook Press, 1991.

Bruns, Roger. *Thomas Jefferson.* New York: Chelsea House, 1986.

Dangerfield, George. *Defiance to the Old World: The Story of the Monroe Doctrine.* New York: Putnam, 1970.

Dwyer, Frank. *John Adams.* New York: Chelsea House, 1989.

Falkner, Leonard. *For Jefferson and Liberty: The United States in War and Peace, 1800–1815.* New York: Knopf, 1972.

Gaines, Ann Graham. *The Louisiana Purchase in American History.* Berkeley Heights, NJ: Enslow Publishers, 2000.

Hakim, Joy. *The New Nation.* New York: Oxford University Press, 1992.

Hauptly, Dennis. *"A Convention of Delegates": The Creation of the Constitution.* New York: Atheneum, 1987.

Hilton, Suzanne. *A Capital Capital City.* New York: Atheneum, 1992.

Hoig, Stan. *A Capital for the Nation.* New York: Cobblehill Books, 1990.

Malone, Mary. *James Madison.* Springfield, NJ: Enslow Publishers, 1997.

Marrin, Albert. *George Washington and the Founding of a Nation.* New York: Dutton Children's Books, 2001.

Meltzer, Milton. *George Washington and the Birth of Our Nation.* New York: Franklin Watts, 1986.

Meltzer, Milton. *Thomas Jefferson, the Revolutionary Aristocrat.* New York: Franklin Watts, 1991.

Old, Wendie C. *James Monroe.* Springfield, NJ: Enslow Publishers, 1998.

Stefoff, Rebecca. *The War of 1812.* New York: Benchmark Books, 2001.

Steins, Richard. *A Nation Is Born: Rebellion and Independence in America, 1700–1820.* New York: Twenty-First Century Books, 1993.

Vaughan, Harold C. *The Constitutional Convention of 1787: The Beginning of Federal Government in America.* New York: Franklin Watts, 1976.

WEB SITES

The Web sites listed here were in existence in 2003–2004 when this book was being written. Their names and/or locations may have changed since then.

In general, when using the Internet to do research on a history topic, you should use caution. You will find numerous Web sites that are very attractive to look at and appear to be professional in format. Proceed with caution, however. Many, even the best ones, contain errors. Some Web sites even insert disclaimers or warnings about mistakes that may have made their way into the site. In the case of primary sources, the builders of the Web site often transcribe previously published material, good or bad, accurate or inaccurate. Therefore, you have to judge the content of *all* Web sites. This requires a critical eye.

A good rule for using the Internet as a resource is always to compare what you find in Web sites to several other sources such as librarian- or teacher-recommended reference works and major works of scholarship. By doing this, you will discover the many different versions of history that exist.

www.historychannel.com/foundingbrothers/
The online companion to the History Channel's four-hour documentary *Founding Brothers* focuses on the early national period, with a time line and biographies.

www.archives.gov/exhibit_hall/charters_of_freedom/constitution/constitution.html/
Maintained by the National Archives and Records Administration, this site includes the text of the Constitution as well as biographies of the people who developed it.

http://murray.lamar.edu/rtest/amhis.htm#enp

This American history reference site has a section devoted to the Early National Period of 1783–1830, with material on the Constitutional Convention, links to primary source documents by many American authors and travelers in America, and online archives of papers by the Federalists and anti-Federalists.

www.militaryheritage.com/1812.htm

This War of 1812 Web site has a large collection of online images and many links to other useful sites.

www.history.rochester.edu/canal/

Maintained by the Department of History of the University of Rochester in New York, this site contains information about the Erie Canal, including a time line, maps, information about canal boats, and links to other sites.

www.law.ou.edu/hist/

The University of Oklahoma's College of Law maintains this online library of historical documents, including presidential addresses, treaties, newspaper articles, and more from the period 1783–1830.

Index

Page numbers for illustrations are in boldface

abolitionists, **69**, 74-76, **75**
Adams, John, 9-11, **9**, **10**, 22, 23, 38
    death of, 35-37
Adams, John Quincy, 24, 50
African Americans. *see* slavery
Age of Reason, 5
Alien and Sedition Acts, 57-59
American affairs, **52**, 53-54
    Alien and Sedition Acts, 57-59
    creation of Washington, DC, 55-57, **56**
    Lewis and Clark expedition, 59-61
    Supreme Court and states' rights, 63-67, **65**
    "The Dangers of American Liberty," 62-63
Ames, Fisher, 62-63
Anti-Federalists, xviii, 2, 17-19, 22
Anti-Republicans, 26-28
antislavery movement, **69**, 70
Articles of Confederation, xvi-xvii
arts and sciences, 81-82
    American writers and playwrights,
      80, 88-91, **89**
    America's first museum, 85-86, **86**
    botanist, 82-85, **84**
    cotton gin, 87-88

Bank of the United States, 64
Barbary pirates, **xix**, 45-47, **46**
Barker, James Nelson, 88-90
Bartram, William, 82-85, **84**
Beecher, Catherine, 102-104, **102**
Bill of Rights, 2, 17
Burr, Aaron, 23-24

capital, national, creation of, **52**, 54,
    55-57, **56**
Capitol (building), 54
checks and balances, governmental
    system of, 8
Civil War, 70
Clark, William, 54, 59-61
Clinton, De Witt, **92**
Constitution, U.S.

amendments to, 3, 24
    Benjamin Franklin on, 11-14, **12**, **13**
    Constitutional Convention of 1787, xvii, 1-2,
      11, 21, 22, 64, 70, 71
    critics of, 17-19, **18**
    need for a new Constitution, 3-5
    ratification of, 3
    signing of, xxiv
Constitution vs. the *Guerrière*, 47-50, **49**
Continental Army, 3
Continental Congress, 54
Cooper, James Fenimore, **80**, 90-91
cotton gin, **82**, 87-88

David Walker's Appeal , 72, **73,** *74*
Decatur, Stephen, 45-47, **46**
Declaration of Independence, 3
democratic government, John Adams on, 9-11,
    9, **10**
Democratic-Republicans, 22
Descartes, René, 5
Diderot, Denis, 5

education, and role of women, 102-104, **102**
electoral college, 21-22
Enlightenment movement, 5-8, **7**
enterprise, American, 93-94
    Englishwoman describes Americans,
      97-99, **98**
    Erie Canal, **92**, 104-107, **105**
    ice trade, 99-101
    improving education, 102-104, **102**
    women of the Lowell factories, 94-96, **95**
Erie Canal, **92**, 104-107, **105**
Everett, Edward, 35-37
executive branch of government, 8, 21

factory workers, 94-96, **95**
The Federalist, 2, 14-16, **15**
Federalists, xviii, 2, 3, 14, 22-23, 24, 26-28,
    32, 62
Ford, Henry, 87

forming a new government, xxiv, 1-3
    Benjamin Franklin on the Constitution, 11-14,
        12, **13**
    Enlightenment movement, 5-8, 7
    The Federalist, 14-16, **15**
    John Adams on democratic government,
        8-11, **9**, **10**
    Mercy Otis Warren, 17-19, **18**
    the need for a new Constitution, 3-5, **4**
Fort McHenry, **39**
Fourth of July, **xiv**, **36**
    deaths of Adams and Jefferson on, 35-37
France
    conflict between U.S. and, xviii
    Jay Treaty and French interests, 38, 43,
        57-58
    Louis XVI and Marie Antoinette, **13**
Franklin, Benjamin, xxiv, 2, 38, 82
    on U. S. Constitution, 11-14, **12**, **13**
French Revolution, 6, 32
Freneau, Philip, 26, 104-107

Garrison, William Lloyd, 74-76, **75**
Great Britain
    British in Northwest Territory, 40-43, **42**
    colonies and, xv, xvi
    conflicts between U.S. and, 38, 40, 53
    Constitution vs. the *Guerrière*, 47-50, **49**
    Jay Treaty and British interests, 43-45, 57
    War of 1812, xviii, **39**, 40, 47

Hall, Edwin Basil, 99-101
Hamilton, Alexander, 2, 22-23, **23**, 54
    Virginia and Kentucky Resolutions letter,
        29-31, **30**
Henry, Patrick, 2
House of Representatives, U.S., 24, 70
Hughes, Thomas, 41-43

ice trade, 99-101
impressment, 40
international affairs, 38, **39**, 40
    Barbary pirates, **xix**, 45-47, **46**
    Constitution vs. the *Guerrière*, 47-50, **49**
    Jay Treaty, 43-45, **44**, 57
    Monroe Doctrine, 50-51, **51**
    war in the Northwest Territory, 40-43, **42**
inventors, American, 87-88

Jay, John, 2, 14-16
    Jay Treaty, 43-45, **44**, 57
Jefferson, Thomas, 2, 23, 24, 26, 29, 82
    and creation of Washington, DC, 55-57, **56**
    death of, 35-37

first inaugural address, 31-35, **32**
    Lewis and Clark expedition, 59
    Louisiana Purchase, 54
    slavery issue, 70
    trade embargo, 38, 40
judicial branch of government, 8

Kentucky Resolutions, 29-31

Larcom, Lucy, xxi-xxii, **xxii**, 95-96
legislative branch of government, 8
L'Enfant, Pierre Charles, 55
Lewis and Clark expedition, 54, 59-61
Lewis, Meriwether, 54, 59-61
Locke, John, 6-8, 7
Louisiana Purchase, 54, **60**
Louisiana Territory, 54, 59
Lowell, Francis Cabot, 94
Lowell girls (factory workers), 94-96, **95**

Madison, James, 23, 24, 26-29, **27**, 29
Malvin, John, 77-79, **79**
Marshall, John, 63-67, **65**
Mason, George, 71-72, **71**
Monroe, James, 24, **60**
    Monroe Doctrine, 50-51, **51**
Montesquieu, Charles Louis de Secondat, 8
museum, America's first, 85-86, **86**

National Gazette, 26-28, 104-105
Native Americans
    in Northwest Territory, 41-42
    Oto Indians, 59-61
    Pocahontas, 88-90, **89**
naturalists, American, 81, 82-85, **84**
Nicholas, John, 58-59
Northwest Territory, 40-43, **42**

Orne, William B., 47-49

Peale, Charles Willson, 85-86, **86**
Philadelphia (U.S. warship), 45-47, **46**
pirates, Barbary, **xix**, 45-47, **46**
play, early American, 88-90, **89**
political parties, formation of, 22-23, **23**
presidents and parties
    Alexander Hamilton, 29-31, **30**
    deaths of Adams and Jefferson, 35-37
    establishment of the presidency, 21-24
    George Washington, **20**, 24-26
    James Madison, 26-29, **27**
    Thomas Jefferson, 31-35, **32**

Quakers, 68, 70

Republican Party, xviii, 22, 23, 24, 32
    James Madison's Republican views, 26-29, **27**
republicanism, 17
Revolutionary War, xv, xvi, xviii, xxiii, 6, 35,
    40, 68, 81, 88, 93
Roper, Moses, 76-77
Rousseau, Jean-Jacques, 5
Rush, Benjamin, 3-5, **4**

Sedgwick, Theodore, 29
Sedition Act, 57-59
Shays, Daniel, 53
shipping industry, U.S., 45
slavery, 68, **69**, 70
    born into, 76-77
    condemnation of, 71-72, **71**
    crusade against, 74-76, **75**
    escaping, 77-79, **79**
    injustice of, 72-74, **73**
Society of Friends (Quakers), 68, 70
Stowe, Harriet Beecher, 102
Supreme Court, U.S., and states' rights, 63-67, **65**

taxation issues, xviii, 53, 64
"The Dangers of American Liberty" (essay),
    62-63

The Indian Princess (play), 88-90, **89**
The Liberator (newspaper), 74-76, **75**
three branches of government, 8
time line, New Republic, 108-109
trade embargo, 38
Treaty of Paris, xv, 40
Trollope, Frances, 97-99, **98**

vice presidency, 21, 22, 23-24
Virginia and Kentucky Resolutions, 29-31
Voltaire, 5

Walker, David, 72-74, **73**
War of 1812, xviii, **39**, 40, 47
Warren, Mercy Otis, 17-19, **18**
Washington, DC, creation of, **52**, 55-57, **56**
Washington, George, xvii, xxiv, 2, **20**, 22, **33**, 35,
    55, 85
    Farewell Address, 24-26
White House, **52**
Whitney, Eli, 82, 87-88
women, American
    education and role of, 102-104, **102**
    Englishwoman describes Americans, 97-99, **98**
    factory workers, 94-96, **95**
writers and playwrights, American, **80**, 88-91, **89**

ABOUT THE AUTHOR

Rebecca Stefoff has written many books about American history, with special attention to the Colonial period and the exploration and settling of the West. She now makes her home in Portland, Oregon, but has lived in the Midwest and on the East Coast. In whatever part of the country she has lived or traveled, she has always enjoyed visiting historic sites and historical museums. You can find out more about Rebecca Stefoff and her books on her Web page: www.rebeccastefoff.com